BEYOND COINCIDENCE

BEYOND COINCIDENCE

God Moments Amid Life's Challenges

Volume 1

Shirley R. Luckadoo

XULON PRESS

Xulon Press
2301 Lucien Way #415
Maitland, FL 32751
407.339.4217
www.xulonpress.com

Paperback ISBN-13: 978-1-6628-1233-0
Hard Cover ISBN-13: 978-1-6628-1234-7
Ebook ISBN-13: 978-1-6628-1235-4

Dedication

This book is dedicated to the King of the Universe in his three persons—Father, Son, and Holy Spirit. It is only through Him and for His purposes that I write. Thank you, dear Abba, Precious Savior, Wonderful Counselor.

"For in him we live and move and exist. As some of your own poets have said, 'We are his offspring.'" (Acts 17:28)

I further thank my wonderful family for their love and support. They are all precious to me—a true gift from God, our Creator. Thank you, dear Gerald (in heaven), Jeff, Stephanie, Luke, Hayley, Lauren, Jon, Kandee, Kaitlyn, Jonathon, Garrett (in heaven), Joe, and Heather. I am blessed beyond measure to have all of you in my life.

Table of Contents

Preface

Although the Holy Spirit prompted me for years to write, it took a potentially fatal car accident to get me to slow down enough to begin to record the many God moments in my every day, ordinary life. As I took time to wait, listen, and open my eyes, I saw His mighty presence all around me in the magical and the mundane, the wondrous and the worrisome.

Beyond Coincidence: God Moments Amid Life's Challenges, Volume 1 is a collection of some of those moments. Grouped by category, each vignette concludes with a challenge to you, the reader, to examine your own life and look for similar God moments. My goal is to offer comfort and challenge to others in accordance with the Scriptures by sharing what the Lord has revealed to me in all kinds of circumstances. As Paul wrote,

"Blessed [gratefully praised and adored] be the God and Father of our Lord Jesus Christ, the Father of mercies and the God of all comfort, who comforts *and* encourages us in every trouble so that we will be able to comfort *and* encourage those who are in any kind of trouble, with the comfort with which we ourselves are comforted by God." (2 Corinthians 1:3-4 AMP)

I pray that you will find help and encouragement through these devotional thoughts and meditations.

Introduction—To help you, the reader, better understand my writing, I have chosen to include my personal story. I hope you will read it before starting the book as I think it will help you see my perspective.

Chapter 1—"God Moments in Sickness and Despair"—shares intimate encounters with God that took place during my months of recuperation and rehabilitation from a broken neck and subsequent back surgery six months later.

Chapter 2—"God Moments in Grief and Tragedy"—offers reflections on God's comfort during times of great loss. In a matter of months, I faced the deaths of my husband, grandson, mother-in-law, brother, sister-in-law, and several friends. God carried my family and me through horrific, gut-wrenching grief and pain. These meditations are based on those times when the Lord met me in my sorrow and gave me His peace during those dark days.

Chapter 3—"God Moments in Addiction and Recovery"—arose out of my work with people in recovery from substance abuse. As co-founder of the Celebrate Recovery Ministry at my church and of Capstone Recovery Center, a transition home for women recovering from substance abuse, I have had many opportunities to see first-hand the power of God in healing the addicted. This chapter shares a few of those observations.

Chapter 4—"God Moments in Times of Spiritual Growth and Spiritual Warfare"—offers insights into some of the problems and opportunities we face because of temptations from Satan and the weaknesses of our own flesh. Pride, fear, and selfishness have been problems for me personally, and I know they have wrecked the lives of many other Christians as well. I have found, though, that good choices in times of temptation can result in tremendous spiritual growth as we allow the Holy Spirit to direct us into His plans for our lives.

Chapter 5—"God Moments When God Calls Us to Service and Obedience"—provides a glimpse of times when the Lord revealed Himself in unexpected ways or called me to some task that seemed impossible or overwhelming.

Chapter 6—"God Moments During Special Occasions and Holidays"—tells of times when the presence of the Holy Spirit was palpable amid the bustle of vacations, birthdays, Christmas, Easter, etc. Such powerful encounters with the Divine intensified the joy and happiness associated with those holiday events.

Chapter 7—"God Moments in Daily Living"—speaks of divine encounters during the ordinary, mundane, every-day activities of life. Whether fretting over taxes, worrying about finances, or trying to make tough decisions, I have found that the Holy Spirit is always there, just waiting for us to call out to Him.

I pray that you will be blessed indeed as you read *Beyond Coincidence: God Moments Amid Life's Challenges,* Volume 1. Except for Chapter 1 which is best read in sequence, the remaining chapters and meditations can be read in any order.

"May the LORD bless you
and protect you.
May the LORD smile on you
and be gracious to you.
May the LORD show you his favor
and give you his peace." (Numbers 6:24-26)

Introduction

The Broken Road Home

My story begins in a little mill town in rural North Carolina called Cliffside. I was a shy little girl who struggled with insecurity and low self-esteem. For reasons I never fully understood, I felt unattractive, inadequate, and unacceptable. I never felt pretty enough, funny enough, cute enough, smart enough—you name it. I was not enough. I never really liked the "Shirley" that God made me to be.

My mother was a stay-at-home mom when I was young, and I never doubted her love for me. My dad, who owned his own business, was a workaholic who worked six or seven days a week and was absent much of my childhood. Though I know now that he loved me very much, I longed for a closer relationship with him as a child. I had one brother, Ron, 18 months younger than I was. I suppose deep down I was jealous of him since he worked summers and weekends with Dad while I stayed home with Mom.

I began at an early age to wear a mask—to try to get people to consider me "acceptable." I had a mask for every occasion.

My family did not attend church regularly, but my parents would allow me to attend various church events. When I was 9, thanks to some godly women at Cliffside Baptist Church, I made a profession of faith and was baptized. I remember it vividly, and I've never doubted that experience. I accepted Jesus as my Savior with the mind of a 9-year-old. I wanted someone to love me and accept me. The Bible said God did, but I still felt inadequate. I never understood His unconditional love since people in our world love very conditionally.

I married the love of my young life at 18. His name was Gerald—Gerry to most people. He was my opposite. His family were church goers. He was handsome, funny, outgoing—all the things that, in my eyes, I was not. We went to college. Graduated. Set out to begin the "perfect" life, whatever that meant.

Our families had secrets, though, that nobody talked about; and my extended family was plagued with alcoholism and codependency—even though I did not know what codependency was until much later in my life. I saw the devastation of alcohol and wanted no part of it; but one evening we were attending our first big party after college, and I was offered my first drink. Rather than say "no," I took it. I did not want to appear less than "perfect" in the eyes of Gerry's new employer—you know, that mask? Little did I know that this first flirtation with alcohol would begin a walk down a road that should have been straight and narrow but would eventually become wide, crooked, and broken.

I knew better, but I wanted to do things MY way. Our problems often start with rebellion—with wanting to do things our own way. I had seen firsthand the problems caused by alcohol abuse, but I wanted to fit in.

A few months later I learned we were pregnant with our first child. We were ecstatic. To our utter dismay, though, I had a miscarriage on Gerry's birthday—October 11. On October 31, 1966, Gerry was drafted into the Army and headed to Fort Dix, New Jersey. For the first time in my life, I faced situations I could not control. I was devastated.

Seeking to control my destiny, I quit my teaching job and followed Gerry to Fort Dix. He was eventually sent to Seoul, Korea, where dependents were not authorized or encouraged. He sent me a letter, though, and told me to sell the car, buy a plane ticket, and come there—he thought I could get a job. Wow! I'd never even been on a plane. But I did it! Thankfully, I got a job as a secretary for a colonel in the Army. Though I was oblivious, the Lord was looking after us in a foreign country that was still in shambles from the Korean war.

As a couple, we grew up while living abroad. For the first time in our lives, we were totally on our own. We learned to depend on each other. Sadly, though, we also allowed the alcohol problem to take hold.

When we returned home, we spent three months at Fort Hood, Texas, where our first precious little boy—Jeffrey—was born. When Gerry was discharged, we moved to Charlotte where God blessed us with two other little boys—Jonathan and Joseph. We loved them with all our hearts, but someday we would come to fail them as parents.

Like so many other young couples, we set out again to seek "the good life." We wanted good jobs, a nice home, clothes, cars, a beautiful family. What began as a flirtation with alcohol gradually became a bigger and bigger problem. Social events involving alcohol were a part of Gerry's job, and my resolve to never have alcohol in my home had caved. On the surface, things were great. New home, new cars, new clothes, new jobs, beautiful new babies—PERFECT. We had it all—but in the secret recesses of my mind, I still didn't feel good about our lives, or about ME.

We were in church but for all the wrong reasons. In our minds, we were supposed to be there, but we were hypocrites. Remember the story of the prodigal son? That was us. Prodigal sons and daughters. Though we did not leave the church physically, we did spiritually. We had chosen the wrong road—the one that would lead to destruction.

"There is a path before each person that seems right, but it ends in death." (Prov. 14:12) Though I never doubted my salvation, I know now that I was not living the abundant life Jesus promised his followers (John 10:10).

God tried to get our attention and redirect us. I had several wake-up calls. On one of our business-related social events, we were on our way to Myrtle Beach to a golf outing related to Gerry's business. We were stopped at a stoplight in Bennettsville, SC, and a 16-year-old boy plowed through the intersection and hit me in my door. The ambulance came. My biggest fear? Not that I had a broken collar bone and a separated shoulder. No, it was that I would be arrested—for we had been drinking as we drove. Though we weren't charged with anything, I vowed never again. That resolve lasted a few days for I was in love—and my lover's name was Jack Daniels. I had gradually moved from rebellion and defiance to voluntary slavery.

What began as a flirtation with alcohol, possessions, and position—things to help me feel better about myself and deal with stress—had now come to enslave me. Truthfully, they had become my idols.

While I didn't recognize it, I now had several gods. They were all around me; only instead of making me feel better, they were gradually killing me. I felt awful. I was a closet alcoholic, workaholic, codependent, shopaholic with four college degrees and a great job, but I was struggling to keep life together. I was very functional in the eyes of the world, but I was a depressed wreck inside. I would go to church and often spend my time crying.

My world was crumbling. Our once happy home was hell on earth—one we had unknowingly created. It was not until our children, who were then teenagers, began having some serious problems that I faced reality.

Proverbs 14:1 says: "A wise woman builds her home, but a foolish woman tears it down with her own hands."

That's what I was doing. I was tearing down my home brick by brick, and the pile of rubble was about to fall on me. The truth of Matthew 6:24 was sinking in:

"No one can serve two masters. For you will hate one and love the other; you will be devoted to one and despise the other. You cannot serve God and be enslaved to money."

I was broken, scared, and tired of running. I was at my bottom, and I was ready to put all my idols on the altar and ask God to be my only God. I was ready for a change! Like the prodigal daughter, I had to repent and return to the Father of my childhood.

In one evening—an evening spent trying to get a precious loved one out of jail for a DWI—I finally turned to God and committed myself to Him totally. I promised Him that if He would help me, I would give up all my idols and worship Him only.

I reached my bottom. I came to realize that "Shirley" couldn't fix "Shirley," and neither could any of the things she had trusted. Those "things" had all betrayed her. I was in a battle—a battle for my family and my life! The road I had chosen was broken and crooked and was about to lead me right over the cliff of total disaster.

With His help, I left my alcohol addiction behind. Was it easy? NO! It was not. Was He faithful? Yes, He was. "He lifted me out of the slimy pit, out of the mud and mire; he set my feet on a rock and gave me a firm place to stand." (Psalm 40:2 NIV)

Gradually, my other idols fell. We sold our expensive house with the big mortgage and moved to a more modest one. I no longer spent every Saturday shopping for the right clothes and cars.

We moved to Salisbury, North Carolina, and joined Trading Ford Baptist Church. I was finally beginning to understand what God had done for me—He had saved me from ME, and He had saved me from Satan himself. I was FREE. I could not do enough for Him.

No longer was I serving Him out of duty, but now it was out of love and adoration. Though no one except close family knew what was taking place in my life, I was in the process of transformation. Just as an ugly caterpillar turns into a free flying butterfly, I was being transformed. Jesus Christ now filled the chasm that had existed between God and me. I no longer filled the hole in my heart with substances and "stuff," but I was filling it with the King of the Universe.

Five years passed. I'd like to say everything in our personal lives became perfect, but that was not the case. The scriptures tell us, "They sow the wind and reap the whirlwind." (Hosea 8:5 NKJV) That was our situation. While the Lord removes our sin as far as the east is from the west, the consequences of our choices frequently continue. After all, Jesus still has scars on His hands and feet.

We as a family of five faced nine alcohol-related accidents and their subsequent legal problems. Praise God, nobody was seriously injured, but the pain and devastation were still there.

It was the summer of 1999. I was at Ridgecrest—a Baptist camp near Asheville—for a week-long leadership conference. I was excited. I had been asked to serve as the Sunday School director for our church and had spent my own money to go for training.

As I sat looking at the program of week-long activities, however, I was drawn not to the Sunday School training program but to a series of new workshops on leading support group ministries. Instead of attending the first Sunday School meeting, I slipped into the first meeting on support groups. As I listened to the speaker,

I was enthralled. The Lord had redirected me, and I knew this was where I needed to be.

For an entire week, I listened in awe at what the presenters shared; and at the last worship service on Thursday night, I made my way to the altar and committed myself to begin a support group ministry at our church. Little did I know, though, what this would entail.

The following morning as we attended our last training session before we headed home, the leader explained that it was time to "drain our spiritual tanks." She explained that each of us had within us a tank into which we had been piling emotional garbage for years.

These tanks were full, and we needed to empty them. She likened it to an infected area deep within us that had become full of gangrene and needed draining for healing to take place. She also reminded us of the words of James—that we were to "confess our sins to each other and pray for each other so that we might be healed." (James 5:16)

WOAH! Red flags went up! An alarm blared in my head! Confess our sins to each other? NO! That was ever so scary—for I had a secret—one that I had carried for years, and I didn't want to tell it to anyone. It was in the past—and that's where it needed to stay—buried.

I thought I would choke as I tearfully told my story. Somehow, though, for the first time in my life, I removed my mask for a few minutes and got honest. It was exceedingly difficult; but it was also very freeing. I returned home and followed through on my promise to try to begin a support group ministry. It was not easy.

I was in a real battle—not just with people but with unseen demons—with the Prince of Darkness himself.

More and more I wanted to serve God. I had begun to keep a journal when I went into recovery, and I loved sitting in the early morning hours with my notebook and my Bible, and spending time talking with God. A scripture passage I had heard at Ridgecrest resonated in my mind. Isaiah 61:1-3 called to me. Though the passage is talking about Jesus, it seemed to call me to be His hands and feet:

> "The Spirit of the Sovereign Lord is upon me,
> for the Lord has anointed me
> to bring good news to the poor.
> He has sent me to comfort the brokenhearted
> and to proclaim that captives will be released
> and prisoners will be freed.
> He has sent me to tell those who mourn
> that the time of the Lord's favor has come,
> and with it, the day of God's anger against
> their enemies.
> To all who mourn in Israel,
> he will give a crown of beauty for ashes,
> a joyous blessing instead of mourning,
> festive praise instead of despair.
> In their righteousness, they will be like great oaks
> that the Lord has planted for his own glory."

The more time I spent with Him, the more I longed for Him. Like the psalmist speaks of a "deer panting for water," so I sought God with a thirst more demanding than any of my previous addictions. I began to see my call as that of a spiritual arborist—one who would help others grow into oaks of righteousness and become followers of Jesus with spiritual roots so deep that nothing would ever blow them over.

Gradually, the Lord led me to leave my wonderful job and the trappings attached to it and go to the seminary. My broken road was becoming straight and narrow—and I loved it! We moved to Spartanburg, SC, where I pastored a tiny church for two years. When I graduated from the seminary with an M.Div. degree, we moved home, and I was at a loss for what to do with myself. I prayed and told God he would have to send someone to knock on my door and tell me what to do, for in my eyes I was too old to be of much use in traditional church roles.

To my surprise, a few days later we did have a knock at the door. It was Pastor Mike Motley, our former pastor. He told us he had a group of people who wanted to begin a ministry called Celebrate Recovery—would we come and help get it started. We had come full circle. That was November 2005. We returned to Trading Ford and became the new ministry leaders for CR. Still involved in the ministry today, I am convinced that our involvement blessed us far more than we ever blessed the people who found healing through the ministry. I am also certain that it was God's grace and CR that helped Gerry finally overcome his battle with alcohol, and I began to deal with my codependency.

Following the founding of CR, we also were blessed to help begin a prison ministry at the Women's Prison in Troy and then to help found Capstone Recovery Center, a recovery ministry for women dealing with substance abuse. Most recently, I have accepted the volunteer position of Executive Director for Hope House, a transition home for women who have completed a recovery program but need a safe place to live while they find employment and rebuild broken relationships. God has been faithful to use our messes for his glory, and what joy that brings!

My relationship with God has deepened. I love Him, I adore Him, I fear Him in the sense that I hold Him in utmost awe and respect. My life has been transformed! I have put away my idols and take delight in worshipping the one, true God. With David, the Psalmist, I rejoice:

"I waited patiently for the LORD to help me,
and he turned to me and heard my cry.
He lifted me out of the pit of despair,
out of the mud and the mire.
He set my feet on solid ground
and steadied me as I walked along." (Psalm 40:1-3)

Does that mean I'm perfect? Far from it. The longer I spend with Him, the more I am aware of my shortcomings, but the more keenly I am aware of how He forgives me and uses me anyway. Like Paul, I still do things I don't want to do and fail to do things I should; but praise God, He loves me anyway! My mess has become His message!

Does that mean my road has been smooth since 1999? No, I've had some very rough spots. In the spring of 2015, Gerry, the love of my life, began showing signs that something was terribly wrong.

He began to have trouble walking and thinking. My once brilliant husband could no longer add simple numbers. Already on dialysis, he was diagnosed with hydrocephalus—fluid on the brain. But before he could have surgery, he was at our weekly CR meeting when he fell in the churchyard with a brain hemorrhage. For the next six months, he was in and out of hospitals with various complications. On October 23, he had emergency surgery for what turned out to be peritonitis—an infection in the abdomen. He never left the hospital until he came home with Hospice on January 1, 2016, to go home to heaven. He passed away on January 10, 2016.

During that time, I came to appreciate the 23rd Psalm in a new way. I walked through the valley of death with my beloved, and the Lord took care of us both.

"Even when I walk
through the darkest valley,
I will not be afraid,
for you are close beside me." (Psalm 23:4)

The Lord carried my family through the grief of losing Gerry only to face the death of my 22-year-old grandson Garrett in a very tragic shooting accident on June 25, 2017. Of all the grief I have experienced, that was the most devastating.

Following Garrett's death in June, I had a near-fatal automobile accident the following October and suffered a broken neck. Since then, I lost my brother Ron and my sister-in-law Gail (Gerry's sister whom I loved like a sister), both to lung cancer. I walked around in a state of shock, and it finally dawned on me that I was the last survivor in my generation. Most recently, I have been diagnosed with breast cancer and have faced surgery and radiation. Praise God, it was treatable, and today I am cancer free!

It was during the three months of recovery from my broken neck that I began to get serious about writing. The Lord had called me to write years earlier, but I had always postponed it—too busy. Well, the Lord sat me down for three months and ensured that I had plenty of time to write. The joy of serving Him in this new way has brought profound healing and blessings beyond belief.

No, the road is not always smooth for any of us. We will all experience ups and downs—highs and lows. Yet I am convinced that "No eye has seen, no ear has heard, and no mind has imagined the things that God has prepared for those who love him." (1 Cor. 2:9).

I have been blessed with three wonderful sons, three precious daughters-in-law, five beautiful grandchildren—one who lives in heaven, a restored marriage, and a shared ministry. My husband, Gerry, was my ministry partner in Celebrate Recovery for 10 years. Now my son Jon and daughter-in-law Kandee have picked up where he left off. Today I am reasonably healthy and pain free. The doctor says that my treatment for breast cancer should be "a bump in the road." What more could one ask for!

My calling here on earth is still summed up in Isaiah 61:1-3. My job, until He calls me home to join my husband and family in heaven, is to be faithful. To listen to His call. To keep on keeping on! In return I have the assurances of Romans 8:38-39: "And I am convinced that nothing can ever separate us from God's love. Neither death nor life, neither angels nor demons, neither our fears for today nor our worries about tomorrow—not even the powers of hell can separate us from God's love. No power in the sky above or in the earth below—indeed, nothing in all creation will ever be able to separate us from the love of God that is revealed in Christ Jesus our Lord."

Thanks for allowing me to share my story. I hope you have been blessed by reading what the Lord has done in my life and that you are further blessed by reading my first book, ***Beyond Coincidence: God Moments Amid Life's Challenges, Volume 1.***

Chapter One

God Moments in Sickness and Despair

Look to the Lord and his strength;
seek his face always.
Psalm 105:4

The Still Small Voice

"The faithful love of the Lord never ends! His mercies never cease. Great is His faithfulness; His mercies begin afresh each morning. The Lord is good to those who depend on him, to those who search for him. So it is good to wait quietly for salvation from the Lord." (Lamentations 3:22-26)

October 23, 2017, 12:50 p.m. I sat waiting to pull out of a parking lot after enjoying lunch with a good friend. A large truck came closer as he tried to pull into the lot where I sat. Thinking I'd give him more room, I pulled forward—failing to see a car coming around him. That split-second decision almost cost me my life as the oncoming vehicle barreled into my car just behind my seat.

I realized from the moment of impact that my neck was injured. People arrived wanting to help me out of the car, but I remained glued to my seat. An internal voice kept saying, "Don't move! Don't move! Don't move!" As my voice screamed and cried, "Help me, Jesus! Help me," the Still Small Voice whispered, "Don't move!" and I obeyed.

Paramedics arrived, stabilized my neck, and loaded me in the ambulance. A CT scan at Rowan Medical Center revealed a fractured C-2 vertebra. As the emergency room doctor delivered the diagnosis, I perceived its seriousness when my daughter-in-law, Kandee, who is a nurse, turned white and whispered, "Don't move, Mama! Don't move!"

I would learn later that a broken C-2 is called a hangman's fracture because it is the bone that breaks when a person is hanged. It was also the source of permanent paralysis for Superman actor Christopher Reeves and countless other accident victims. A chiropractor would tell me months later that only a small percentage of accident victims survive this injury without death or paralysis.

The ER doctor announced that I would need to be moved to a trauma center better equipped to care for spinal injuries. As the attendants strapped me to a back board and loaded me in the ambulance, I became keenly aware of the "Still Small Voice" from the moments after the accident whispering, "Don't move!"

The ER staff told me more than once that I had been "very smart" to sit still in the car, but I remembered that my first instinct at the time of impact was to jump out and get away. Rather, that "Still Small Voice"—the Holy Spirit, I believe—kept warning me, "Don't move." Psalm 46:10 (NKJV) echoed in my head, "Be still and know that I am God."

After they loaded me in the ambulance a second time, two nurses who would accompany me introduced themselves. Angels in disguise, they took care of me spiritually and physically. Having to ride on a backboard with a broken neck in the back of an ambulance is intimidating in itself; but to make matters worse, there were tornado warnings and heavy winds brewing. The driver kept commenting to the nurses that the winds were making it difficult to drive. The nurses calmly explained what would happen upon arrival at the ER in Winston-Salem.

Nearing the hospital, one of the nurses commented that despite the heavy winds and the rush hour traffic, we had made record time. I felt like Moses must have felt when the Lord parted the Red Sea! When the doors swung open and they prepared me to leave the vehicle, one of the "angels" commented, "I will pray for you—and I mean it!" What a blessing!

When we entered the Emergency Room, a parade of doctors and nurses greeted me. While I lay there on my back unable to see anything but the ceiling, faceless voices came and went. One of those faceless voices announced that I was headed for a CT scan.

Fear gripped me as visions of a previous MRI flooded my mind. Since I am claustrophobic, I was terrified at being encased in a tube.

The Lord and I began to discuss this dilemma, and He reminded me of a very recent conversation I had had with my sister-in-law, Gail, who told me the only way she got through an MRI was by singing hymns and quoting scriptures to herself. Thus, began a silent time of personal worship, praise, and thanksgiving as I closed my eyes and went through what seemed like an eternity in a coffin. Psalm 23:4 came to mind: "Even when I walk through the darkest valley, I will not be afraid, for you are close beside me." I peeped through one eye for one brief second and saw that someone had put an image of flowers on the ceiling of the "casket." How appropriate, I thought!

My silent singing and praying intensified. "Jesus Paid It All" and "Jesus Loves Me" came to my remembrance. What reassurance! My Abba—my Daddy—was there. An amazing sense of calm came over me. The Lord had met me in the storms—the real ones and the imagined ones—and calmed them for me. Just as he calmed the seas for the terrified disciples (Luke 8:22-25), so he had calmed my fears. He was with me—whatever came my way!

On return to the ER, my pastor Mike Motley and my family arrived. One by one they came to encourage me. How precious each visitor was! At one point, my daughter-in-law Heather and I were alone in my little "room" which was nothing more than a curtained off area with other patients on either side. A commotion began—someone screamed in pain—cursing the doctors—begging for mercy. Then another voice on my other side began to scream even louder.

A nurse alerted us that we were on lock-down—that if Heather should leave, she could not come back in and neither could anyone else. Thank the Lord, she assured me she would stay, for I was helpless, strapped down to the bed without even a call bell. It was in some ways terrifying, but to my surprise, I remained calm. We would later learn that the two "voices" were gunshot victims, and their presence—along with several police officers—was the reason for the lock-down.

Over the next few hours, the trauma doctors consulted with the spine doctors, and they finally agreed sometime around midnight that I would go not to ICU but to a regular room, My son Joe and his wife Heather would spend the night. Other family would go home to rest up for their turns with Mama.

It was a long night! More tests. More X-rays. A little sleep from 5 a.m. until 7 a.m. Shift change. New nurses. The day drifted by. Finally, though, I got good news! To everyone's utter surprise, I was going home! Prayers had been answered!

They bound my neck in a cervical collar, gave the list of "Do Nots" to my son Jon and his wife Kandee, and we were homeward bound!

The not so good news? I would wear the cervical collar for at least three months. I could not drive until they removed the collar. I would need help with bathing, housework, self- care, etc. The stark realization came that if it weren't for precious family, I'd be headed to a nursing home.

Then another revelation came to me. The Lord had spared me, but His reasons were unclear. Why had He left me among the living? Tears welled up as I remembered the tragedies I had already endured over the preceding few months. First, I had struggled through the lengthy illness and death of my dear husband Gerald 20 months previously, and then the tragic death of my grandson Garrett less than four months ago. Why was I not headed to see them in heaven?

Against the backdrop of all the heartbreak I had recently encountered, I realized I had some new choices to make. How would I respond to yet another monumental challenge? Would I continue to rely on the King of the Universe to carry me when I could not take care of myself? Or would I give in to despair?

In contemplating my dilemma, I was reminded of Elijah's encounter with God (1 Kings 19:11-12) when the Lord spoke to him in a "Still Small Voice." Elijah was hiding out in a cave, convinced the Lord had deserted him. He was scared and depressed. I could certainly identify! The Lord ministered to Elijah. He cared for him in his time of need.

I, too, had heard the Still Small Voice. I would obey. I was confident that the Lord would provide for me as well. In retrospect, I realize the Lord has a sense of humor, for I had no choice! He had me where he wanted me—still—an unfamiliar place for a workaholic Martha-type personality! (Luke 10:38-42)

As I mulled over my situation, I began to consider that perhaps it was time for me to get serious about writing a blog or maybe a book that he had been prompting me to write for years. Perhaps now I would have time—and inclination—to listen and follow and write.

CHALLENGE: What about you? Have you ever had an experience when you knew that the Lord had saved you from disaster? If so, I challenge you to do two things.

First, get a journal—a simple notebook will do—and write about the event. Listen for the Lord's still small voice as you write.

Second, celebrate the miracle by telling the Lord and others about it as you bring glory to Him.

Father God, Divine Healer, we know that you told the demoniac whom you healed to, "Go home to your friends, and tell them what great things the Lord has done for you, and how He has had compassion on you." (Mark 5:19 NKJV)

May we do likewise.

No Fear

"Don't worry about anything; instead, pray about everything. Tell God what you need, and thank him for all he has done. Then you will experience God's peace, which exceeds anything we can understand. His peace will guard your hearts and minds as you live in Christ Jesus." (Philippians 4:6-7)

Grim faces and hushed voices greeted me as most of the family awaited my arrival from the hospital. I had just been released to go home after a car wreck that left me with a broken neck.

Fear was etched on their faces. A recliner was moved to my bedroom—my new "bed." Two dear daughters-in-law, Stephanie and Kandee, escorted me to it. I could not walk on my own. My speech was garbled, and I was told later I was talking out of my head. Effects of morphine wearing off, I imagine.

I remember asking my family to find my deceased husband Gerald's walker as I staggered down the hall and sat down carefully on my new "bed." I had often said I could not sleep on my back, but I did—blessed sleep—and in a recliner!

When I slowly awoke the following morning, I managed to stand up and start down the hall toward the kitchen with coffee on my mind! My son Jeff, my night "nurse," met me. "It's a miracle!" he exclaimed, excited but concerned that I was walking on my own. He and Stephanie moved into action preparing coffee and breakfast—taking over MY old job!

Thus, began the first full day of being home from the hospital, and "reality" was slowly setting in. The "Do Not" list I had received from my doctors would mean a whole new lifestyle for the next three months. I really was going to have to "be still!" I had been told not to drive, not to pick up over eight pounds, not to lean over, not to do much of anything except allow others to take care of my needs. As a "descendant" of Martha in the scriptures (Luke 10:38-42)—a workaholic who thrives on activity—what was I to do? Again, the Still Small Voice reminded me, "Be still and know that I am God!" (Psalm 46:10) The Lord meant business! I was to be still, listen, and obey!

Though I did not blame Him or think He had caused my accident, He had allowed it; and I believed there was a purpose in it, even if I could not yet discern "why." My job was to fulfill that purpose, whatever it was.

Jesus had told Martha that Mary, her sister, had it right—that sitting at His feet and listening to Him were more important than frantic activity. It was time for me to become more like Mary. And believe it or not, I was at peace with it! Jesus had been with me in my car as He told me, "Don't move," when I was hit by an oncoming car. He had been there in that ambulance as the winds blew around us. He had been with me in the ER, the CT machines, a lock-down of the emergency room because of a gun fight, the ride home, the night in the recliner—and He would be with me through what lay ahead because He is my Savior, my best Friend, my Provider, my Guide, my Shepherd, my Lord!

He told his disciples in Luke 12:6-7, "What is the price of five sparrows—two copper coins? Yet God does not forget a single one of them. And the very hairs on your head are all numbered. So, don't be afraid; you are more valuable to God than a whole flock of sparrows." In other words, He loves us!

In reflecting on my experiences with fear, I am reminded of what Paul told Timothy: "For God has not given us a spirit of fear and timidity, but of power, love, and self-discipline." (2 Tim. 1:7) I am confident that when fear bubbles up in us, it is not from the Lord but from our own flesh or from Satan. During such times, it is up to us to claim his "power, love, and self-discipline" through the Holy Spirit who resides within us.

I had to tell myself often that I could be still for three months and spend more time listening to the Father. It would be hard, but I knew I could do it!

Challenge: What about you? What are you afraid of? What trials are you facing? Spend some time in communion with God. Write down what you hear Him saying and pray for new direction. Thank Him for His care during dark times.

Thank you, Lord, for taking care of us when we can't take care of ourselves and for giving our lives meaning and purpose during times of sickness and despair.

Joyful in Hard Times

"Dear brothers and sisters, when troubles of any kind come your way, consider it an opportunity for great joy. For you know that when your faith is tested, your endurance has a chance to grow. So, let it grow, for when your endurance is fully developed, you will be perfect and complete, needing nothing."
James 1:2-4

During my three-month recovery from a broken neck, nights at home were long. With a cervical collar wrapped tightly around my neck and instructions never to take it off, I found it difficult to sleep. For three nights, I slept in the recliner my sons had moved into my room. I could not figure out how to move safely into and out of my bed. Finally, with the help of a physical therapist on a YouTube video and my son Jeff, I learned how to lie down and get up. What a challenge!

A new routine emerged. Sleep two hours in bed. Get uncomfortable. Sleep two hours in the chair. Uncomfortable again. Move back to the bed. I was getting tired and grumpy! As I arose on my fifth day at home, I was irritable. Sitting down on my sunporch to begin my daily devotional time, I complained to the Lord that I was tired of the collar, that it was uncomfortable, that I could not sleep, that it itched, blah, blah, and more blahs.

And then the Lord spoke to me very clearly, "Be thankful for that collar. Let it become your new BFF. Recognize that it is embracing you—not choking you! Remember it is keeping you upright at home rather than prone in a hospital bed for months. Work on your attitude!"

And I did—I really tried! I worked hard to develop an attitude of gratitude instead of one of whining and complaining. No, I didn't like the collar, but I can say now that I became thankful for it. 1 Thessalonians 5:16-18 took on a new meaning, "Always be joyful. Never stop praying. Be thankful in all circumstances, for this is God's will for you who belong to Christ Jesus."

Notice it says "in all circumstances" not "for all circumstances." I have found that we can be thankful "in" our circumstances because we have a loving Father who will carry us "through" them.

On my first Sunday back at church, Pastor Mike Motley, pastor at Trading Ford Baptist Church, preached from Psalm 23:4, "He restores my soul." Pastor Mike explained that there is a condition among sheep that renders them helpless—flat on their backs—unable to get back up. These poor animals are called "cast sheep" or "kessing sheep."

Unless the shepherd helps cast sheep back on their feet, they will usually die. Such are we spiritually. When we are flat on our backs in a pit of depression and despair, we need the Good Shepherd Jesus Christ to set us on our feet again or we, too, risk spiritual death as we succumb to unbelief, anger, bitterness, unforgiveness, gloom, and desolation.

When I lay in the hospital flat on my back with my broken neck, I realized how much I had taken for granted. I was a cast sheep—physically and spiritually. Praise God, He stood me up, sent me home, began healing me, and gently corrected me when I was tempted to backslide into the pit! The least I could do was say "Thank you!" with a cheerful attitude!

I could identify with the psalmist:

"Then I realized that my heart was bitter,
and I was all torn up inside.

I was so foolish and ignorant—
I must have seemed like a senseless animal to you.
Yet I still belong to you;
you hold my right hand.
You guide me with your counsel,
leading me to a glorious destiny.
Whom have I in heaven but you?
I desire you more than anything on earth.
My health may fail, and my spirit may grow weak,
but God remains the strength of my heart;
He is mine forever." (Psalm 73:21-26)

As I read and meditated on the psalm, I was reminded of a book by Ann Voskamp that has had a tremendous impact on me. When Ann was five years old, she watched as her younger sister was run over and killed by a delivery truck. Because of this tragedy, a joyless mood of depression seemed to overwhelm her and her family throughout her childhood. As she became a mother herself, she longed for a joy she had never known until an acquaintance challenged her to begin a list of 1,000 gifts. She accepted the challenge, and this simple practice transformed her life and became the basis of her best-selling book, *One Thousand Gifts*.

My previous two years had been challenging. With the passing of my husband Gerry and grandson Garrett within 17 months of each other and then the debilitating accident that had left me with a broken neck, I was keenly aware that it would be very easy to become that "cast sheep" again.

It was almost time for Thanksgiving and Christmas. The upcoming holiday season could be difficult. I prayed, though, that my family could focus on our Lord and Savior, Jesus Christ, and experience the awe of Christmas despite our struggles.

I prayed that my list of 1,000 gifts would include precious memories of past years, delightful moments in the here and now, and hope-filled dreams of the future. Isaiah 43:19 reminded me, "For I am about to do something new. See, I have already begun! Do you not see it? I will make a pathway through the wilderness. I will create rivers in the dry wasteland." Even in the most difficult situations, King Jesus promises us a "future and a hope." (Jeremiah 29:11)

CHALLENGE: What about you? Have you experienced the powerful hand of the Good Shepherd lifting you up from your prone position and setting your feet on solid ground? Have you found unimaginable joy as you developed an attitude of gratitude? Begin a Gratitude List or Journal of things for which you are thankful—big, small, even tiny. Add to it each day. Share your joy with others who may need encouraging.

Precious Savior, our Good Shepherd, thank you for carrying us through difficult circumstances and giving us hope for new beginnings and new futures.

In Search of True Beauty

"People look at outward appearance, but the Lord looks at the heart." (1 Samuel 16:7 NIV)

When I broke my neck and had to wear a cervical collar 24/7, I had many questions from others about how I coped. Did I have to wear the collar when I slept? Yes. Could I take it off to shower? No. Wasn't it annoying? Yes.

One of the most difficult things to get accustomed to, though, was the inability to follow my usual "beauty" regimen. Makeup and hair care were nearly impossible. Even shampooing was a three-person process. I washed my hair in the shower wearing the collar. Then I lay down on the bed for daughter-in-law Kandee to carefully remove the wet collar. Daughter-in-law Heather replaced the wet pads with dry ones so that Kandee could then put back on the dry collar, all without moving my head.

Since my neck always had to remain immobilized, trips to the beauty salon for haircuts and color were pleasures of the past until Kandee and my talented hairdresser, Kathy Tucker, figured out how to help bedraggled looking me. Friday morning, December 1, Kandee held my neck in place while Kathy quickly cut and colored my hair and sent me home for a final shampoo and rinse in my own shower. Different—but effective. I felt like a new person!

As I awkwardly dried and curled my hair and prepared to go to an afternoon funeral, I still saw a chipmunk staring back at me in the mirror—squished-up jaws, new wrinkles emerging above the tight collar encasing my neck, and no makeup except lipstick because it would get on the collar. Not an attractive picture—but one I needed to accept.

Dressed in one of few outfits that would fit over the collar, I climbed in the back of the car with Jon and Kandee and headed for the funeral of 93-year-old Cleo Rosella Mullis Cloninger (Boots), grandmother to my daughter-in-law Stephanie, and a long-time friend of our entire family.

As we entered the church, I could not help but notice the almost packed sanctuary full of people who were there to honor and remember Boots and comfort her husband Bob and the rest of her loved ones. Reverend Noel Sweezy, the first minister to speak, stood, prayed, then asked the congregation to call out words to describe Mama Boots. "Sweet, kind, caring, compassionate, fun loving, always smiling, gentle, humble, soft spoken, lover of children" echoed across the audience.

Then he read 1 Corinthians 13 and asked us to think of the many ways Boots emulated that passage. "Love is patient and kind. Love is not jealous or boastful or proud or rude. It does not demand its own way. It is not irritable, and it keeps no record of being wronged. It does not rejoice about injustice but rejoices whenever the truth wins out. Love never gives up, never loses faith, is always hopeful, and endures through every circumstance." (1 Cor. 13:4-6) Yes, that was the Boots I remembered.

The second minister, Rev. Sonny Reavis, Boots' nephew, shared memories of how Mama Boots had taken him and his sister into her own home for a year when he was eight years old and lavished love and attention on them in ways that transformed their lives. He credited Boots with preparing his heart for his call to ministry as she had showed the love of Christ to him in his young life.

As the beautiful service concluded, I could not help but dab damp eyes when Lauren Luckadoo, Boots' great granddaughter and my own precious granddaughter, lifted glorious praises to our Creator as she sang *How Great Thou Art*. Lauren was the last child Mama Boots had lovingly cared for in her declining years before dementia robbed her of precious memories.

What a tremendous testimony to a life well lived in service to King Jesus!

As we followed the casket out of the service for transport to the cemetery, my mind drifted to the Proverbs 31 woman, a wonderful role model for any Christian.

"Her children stand and bless her. Her husband praises her: There are many virtuous and capable women in the world, but you surpass them all! Charm is deceptive, and beauty does not last; but a woman who fears the Lord will be greatly praised." (Proverbs 31:28-30)

Such was Cleo Rosella "Boots" Mullis Cloninger. She was beautiful physically—but even more so spiritually. What a legacy she left! What an example for younger women to follow.

The following morning as I read devotional thoughts from *Daily Guideposts*, I thought once again of Mama Boots. The focal passage was 1 Peter 3: 3-5, "Don't be concerned about outward beauty...clothe yourselves instead with the beauty that comes from within, the unfading beauty of a gentle and quiet spirit, which is so precious to God. This is how the holy women of old made themselves beautiful. They put their trust in God."

A moment of conviction pierced my heart. Even though I might think I look like a chipmunk, I am a part of "God's masterpiece." He has created us anew in

Christ Jesus, so we can do the good things he planned for us long ago. (Ephesians 2:10)

That Still Small Voice seemed to whisper that He made me, and He was there "as I was woven together in the dark of the womb." (Psalm 139:15)

Further, He would do some repair work and weave my broken bones back together. While I waited, I just needed to concentrate on developing that inward beauty that shone forth in Mama Boots rather than fret too much about looking like a chipmunk. After all, chipmunks are cute, too!

Challenge: What about you? More concerned about outward than inward beauty? Perhaps it's time to concentrate more on eternal rather than temporal qualities. Why not write a brief reflection in your journal and add a few praise items to your gratitude list?

Creator God, forgive us when we fail to see the beauty in your creation, including ourselves, and help us to concentrate on the eternal rather than the temporal.

Thankful for a Broken Neck

"Be thankful in all circumstances, for this is God's will for you who belong to Christ Jesus." (1 Thessalonians 5:18)

After almost three months in a cervical collar for a broken neck, I was excited. This was the day to see the doctor for possible removal of the collar—freedom!

My daughter-in-law Kandee had driven me to the appointment at a doctors' office in Winston-Salem—38

miles from my home. A dear friend, Miriam Ramirez, had also accompanied us.

X-rays were taken. We waited for the results. It was taking forever, or so it seemed!

"What will I do, Lord, if the healing is incomplete?" I silently prayed. "What will I do if I have to remain in this collar for several more weeks or months? What if I have to continue to rely on other people to drive me everywhere and take care of me?"

Quietly I realized I needed to stop the what-ifs. The Lord had carried me this far. I would be o.k. "Well, Lord, I won't like it, but I will continue to do what I have been doing—waiting," I confessed.

Finally, good news! The physician's assistant returned and said I was good to go! Physical therapy would be necessary to ensure mobility, but I was collar free!

Kandee turned to me, tears in her eyes, "I'm so happy I could cry!" she said as Miriam snapped our picture. It had been a long three months!

Next stop: our weekly Celebrate Recovery meeting at Trading Ford Baptist Church.

As I pulled into the church parking lot, my 12-year old granddaughter, Kaity, came running toward me smiling from ear to ear, her long hair bouncing behind her. As she jerked open the door, however, she burst into tears. "What's wrong?" I asked with concern. "Nothing! I'm just so happy!" she responded.

Tears of joy! Welcome tears! Happy tears! We hadn't had many of those lately. It was a good day!

As I entered the Fellowship Building, cheers erupted from my Celebrate Recovery family who had been so faithful to pray for me, encourage me, help me! Such a wonderful "forever family."

Spirits were high as we shared our fellowship meal and headed to the Worship Center.

The praise team led us in a rousing time of worship, and our speaker began to share the lesson. My thoughts, though, were scattered—drifting here and yon. My arduous journey was over. The Divine Physician had spared me from paralysis or death. Gratitude filled my soul! I was incredibly grateful!

Admittedly, being house bound had been a challenge for someone who was constantly on the go, but a glimmer of truth began to dawn on me. In strange ways this time of immobility had also been a great blessing. It was during my convalescence that I had learned what it meant to "Be still and know that I am God." (Psalm 46:10)

An odd sense of anxiety and longing began to creep over me. Did I really want to return to my pre-wreck days—the too busy, bustling days filled often with too much activity, or did I want to continue at the slower pace I had been enjoying since the accident?

I began to realize that I was oddly grateful for my three months of forced stillness. It was during that time that I had finally quieted myself enough to hear the Lord speak to me much more clearly.

It was during that time that I had finally begun to write—something I had wanted to do for years.

It was during that time that I basked in the love and prayers of God's people—Baptists, Methodists, Pentecostals. Notes, letters, visits, calls, e-mails, texts, gifts, and food had overflowed! I was even blessed with not one but two prayer quilts--one from my own Trading Ford Baptist and one from First Baptist Church in Stanley--a church I attended 30 years ago. I was overwhelmed as I experienced the "Church" at its best—praying, loving, supporting, encouraging!

It was during that time that I learned the full extent of the love and faithfulness of my dear family. Without them, I would have spent my convalescence in a nursing home or assisted living facility. What a marvelous blessing they had been! Thank you, Jeff, Steph, Jon, Kandee, Joe, Heather, Kaity, Jonathon, Lauren, Nick, Luke, and Hayley. I love you!

Finally, it was during this time that I, like whirlwind Martha in the scriptures, heard Jesus tell me clearly and lovingly that I needed to be more like my "sister" Mary, who sat at His feet. "There is only one thing worth being concerned about. Mary has discovered it, and it will not be taken away from her." (Luke 10:38-42) Even though my inactivity had been forced, I had learned well that I needed to continue to carve out larger chunks of time to sit with Him—to listen to Him—to learn from Him, and to write about Him.

As my mind returned to the CR meeting, it was already "chip time," the time when people make commitments to start on the road to recovery from some hurt, habit, or hang-up and receive a coin-sized token as a reminder of the commitment.

A sense of calm assurance washed over me as I walked forward and took a blue chip—a beginner's chip. It was time for me to give up my workaholism and commit to continue my journey away from "busyness" and toward sitting with the Savior.

Challenge: What about you? Do you wrestle with workaholic tendencies like Martha? Do you struggle to be still and know God? Have you ever attended a Celebrate Recovery meeting where you could take off your mask, learn more about yourself, and develop a support network? Celebrate Recovery is for all hurts, habits, and hang-ups. Everyone has them. Consider visiting a local Celebrate Recovery. Perhaps you could bless others as they bless you. You can find a list of local ministries at www.celebraterecovery.com, the national website.

Lord, help me to be still in body, mind, and spirit as I listen to YOU and Your ways and seek to obey.

Oh, Lord, Where Are You?

"The faithful love of the Lord never ends! His mercies never cease. Great is his faithfulness; his mercies begin afresh each morning. I say to myself, 'The Lord is my inheritance; therefore, I will hope in him!'" (Lamentations 3:22-24)

On August 1, 2018, only six months after recovering from a broken neck, I was busy sweeping my kitchen when I turned and felt a sting, almost like a little pop, in my lower back. My immediate prayer, "Ooh, Lord, that was not good! I pray I don't have a big problem arise out of that!"

Though I'm positive He heard, and I'm positive He answered, I'm also positive it was just not the way I wanted! In fact, little did I know what a nightmare lay ahead, the second health crisis in less than a year!

I was scheduled to fly to Breckenridge, Colorado, on August 4 for our annual family vacation. Rather than see a doctor before we left, I climbed aboard the plane and took off. A big mistake! By day, I tried to have fun with the family as I put on a happy face. By night, I wallowed in pain, sleeping little, arising in the middle of the night for Aleve, Tylenol, and ice packs. I dug into the Word and cried out to God, but relief did not come.

As the days progressed, my minor injury turned into a bigger and bigger problem. After a few days, the pain steadily increased in my left hip and made its way into my left leg down to my knee. I began to hobble and found it difficult to stand up straight.

Even before I left Breckenridge headed for home, I called for an appointment with my general practitioner as soon as possible upon my return. My usual doctor was not available, and I saw the first person I could, a second mistake. Her diagnosis? Using X-rays taken in 2014, she concluded I had degeneration in my lower spine. Her prescription? Take prednisone for inflammation, hydrocodone to help me sleep, and go to the chiropractor and the physical therapist. After dutifully following her instructions, I was worse. The pain had crept down my leg to my calf.

On August 23 I went back to my GP and saw my usual nurse practitioner who wisely took a new X-ray and diagnosed me with a bulging disk. Her prescription? Muscle relaxers, a Kenalog injection, Tramadol for pain, and more physical therapy. Over the next few days, I became worse. The pain was now into my heel. I could hardly walk and was now stooped over like the Hunchback of Notre Dame.

Because of my ministry to women in addiction to pain killers, I did not want to take narcotics. Over-the-counter medications, however, did little to relieve the spasms. The pain was so severe I was willing to take almost anything prescribed for relief.

I filled my journals with scripture and prayer, but I could no longer think of anything but my discomfort. I could no longer write my blog. I was too self-absorbed with my situation. I learned an important lesson: chronic pain and the related meds are debilitating.

Like Job and his friends, I cried out, "Why?" I did repeated self-examinations for unconfessed sin. I made promises to God that I am now trying to keep. I concluded if my life was going to be one of constant pain, then I was ready to go "home" if the Lord would just call me! He didn't.

Convinced I was under spiritual attack, I began a study of spiritual warfare and what to do when Satan comes calling. I carefully studied Ephesians 6:13-17 and consciously began "putting on my armor" when I staggered in agony out of bed each morning. I imagined I was putting on armor as described in the Scriptures:

"Therefore, put on every piece of God's armor so you will be able to resist the enemy in the time of evil. Then after the battle you will still be standing firm. Stand your ground, putting on the belt of truth and the body armor of God's righteousness. For shoes, put on the peace that comes from the Good News so that you will be fully prepared. In addition to all of these, hold up the shield of faith to stop the fiery arrows of the devil. Put on salvation as your helmet, and take the sword of the Spirit, which is the word of God." (Ephesians 6:13-17)

On September 5, I returned to my GP. She sent me immediately for an MRI and arranged an appointment with a neurosurgeon.

The neurosurgeon and I discussed options and settled on surgery, but my insurance company demanded three weeks to process the paperwork. It devastated me. My life had become a hell of pain and pills, none of which could end the cycle. I couldn't sleep. I couldn't focus. I couldn't stand up straight. I was becoming more and more stooped. My left foot did not want to fully support me.

My children watched all of this, and on September 21, my daughter-in-law Heather, who is a health professional, and my son Joe concluded that something had to be done. They took me to the emergency room. After spending the night waiting to see a doctor, the physician on call did an examination and called my surgeon. Within three hours I finally had the operation. The Lord used the skilled hands of a surgeon to rescue me!

What a blessing! The Lord carried me through the most horrific physical pain I had ever encountered! Today, I am pain free and walking better than I have in months! I am also free of all pain medication, a huge blessing as well!

My first doctor failed me, my insurance carrier initially failed me, but the Lord never failed me! Though I sometimes wondered where he was and why I was suffering, I was reminded of 2 Corinthians 4:8-10:

"We are pressed on every side by troubles, but we are not crushed. We are perplexed, but not driven to despair...We get knocked down, but we are not destroyed. Through suffering, our bodies continue to share in the death of Jesus so that the life of Jesus may also be seen in our bodies." (2 Corinthians 4:8-10)

Paul also penned these encouraging words that we can draw on in times of great distress, "And I am convinced that nothing can ever separate us from God's love. Neither death nor life, neither angels nor demons, neither our fears for today nor our worries about tomorrow—not even the powers of hell can separate us from God's love. No power in the sky above or in the earth below—indeed, nothing in all creation will ever be able to separate us from the love of God that is revealed in Christ Jesus our Lord." (Romans 8:38-39)

Praise God! I am healed and pain free! Though there were times when I was discouraged and distressed, I can rejoice in my Savior! With Job I can say, "Though He slay me, yet will I trust Him." (Job 13:15 NKJV)

Challenge: What about you? Are you struggling today with a debilitating illness? Have you seen and felt the Lord's hand of mercy even though you sometimes can't see past the pain? I pray you hang in there! He is faithful. Claim His promises and record them in a gratitude journal.

Oh, Divine Healer, we cry out to you in our distress and trust that you will care for us and heal our diseases in your time and in your way.

Look What the Lord Has Done!

"It is good to give thanks to the Lord, to sing praises to the Most High." (Psalm 92:1)

After having back surgery in September and experiencing the Lord's healing power, I found Thanksgiving to be extra special. As in most years, it was not uncommon for people to ask, "What are you thankful for this year?'

Without hesitation, I answered, "That I am pain free!" What a wonderful blessing to get out of bed, walk down the hall for my morning coffee, and be pain free! How awesome to go outside unassisted and greet the Lord with outstretched arms!

The previous Thanksgiving, I was housebound from a broken neck I had suffered in an automobile accident. After weeks of physical therapy, I recovered. Then only six months later, I was sweeping my kitchen and injured my back. This very ordinary activity sent me into three more months of dealing with excruciating back pain and surgery and more restrictions.

So when I said I was thankful for getting out of bed pain free, I meant it!

There is a wonderful story in the book of Acts that captured how I felt as we gathered for our traditional Thanksgiving:

"Peter and John went to the Temple one afternoon to take part in the three o'clock prayer service. As they approached the Temple, a man lame from birth was being carried in...When he saw Peter and John about to enter, he asked them for some money.

Peter and John looked at him intently, and Peter said, 'Look at us!' The lame man looked at them eagerly, expecting some money. But Peter said, 'I don't have any silver or gold for you. But I'll give you what I have. In the name of Jesus Christ, the Nazarene, get up and walk!'

Then Peter took the lame man by the right hand and helped him up. And as he did, the man's feet and ankles were instantly healed and strengthened. **He jumped up, stood on his feet, and began to walk! Then, walking, leaping, and praising God, he went into the Temple with them."** (Acts 3:1-8)

Did you notice what the lame man did after he was healed? "Walking, leaping, and praising God, he went into the Temple with them." He was all about praising and worshipping the Lord! That's what I wanted to do!

King David said it quite eloquently in Psalm 103:1-5:

"Let all that I am praise the Lord;
with my whole heart, I will praise his holy name.
Let all that I am praise the Lord;
may I never forget the good things he does for me.
He forgives all my sins
and heals all my diseases.

He redeems me from death
and crowns me with love and tender mercies.
He fills my life with good things. My youth is renewed
like the eagle's!"

Wow! That last verse is significant when you are as old as I am!

With each passing year, I become more aware that our days are numbered, that we have less and less time on this earth to serve and praise the Lord. With my accidents this year, I have also realized how quickly our health can be compromised, severely limiting our mobility and our ability to serve the Lord actively. In a split second, we can be bedridden, unable to care for ourselves much less care for others.

As I entered the Advent season, I wanted to maintain an attitude of gratitude. Through circumstances beyond my control, I had learned to "be still and know that I am God." Psalm 46:10.

Even though the year had been difficult, I said in retrospect that I was thankful for the hard days, for I had grown closer to the Lord and experienced his presence in ways far beyond what I would have experienced had I spent the year in my usual flurry of busyness and activity. I learned what James meant when he wrote, "Dear brothers and sisters, when troubles of any kind come your way, consider it an opportunity for great joy. For you know that then your faith is tested, your endurance has a chance to grow." (James 1:2-3)

There is a wonderful praise and worship song that captured the essence of my thoughts and emotions that Thanksgiving season. Every time I hear it, I want to clap my hands and jump for joy! Recorded by several groups including the Gaithers, the first verse is about the lame man who leaped to his feet and began praising the Lord for what he had done. Verse 2 celebrates a more important healing—a spiritual one whereby we experience his healing from sin and the promise of eternity in heaven.

If you want a great praise song to lift your spirits and get your day off to a good start, check out the You Tube rendition of "Look What the Lord Has Done." It will make your day!

CHALLENGE: What about you? We serve an awesome God. Want to brag on Him? Pray and add to your Gratitude Journal. Share what you wrote with someone else.

Father, help us to be thankful in every season for the gifts you provide and for your tender care and healing during times of sickness.

Words of Encouragement from the Heavens

Your unfailing love, O Lord, is as vast as the heavens; your faithfulness reaches beyond the clouds."
(Psalm 36:5)

Have you ever noticed how the Lord speaks to us in all kinds of amazing ways? One of the most fascinating to me, though, is how he can communicate with us through the heavens if we but look up and listen with our eyes.

Back in October 2017 my brother Ron was hospitalized with complications from lung cancer. Late one afternoon on my way to visit him in Rutherford Hospital, a two-hour drive from my home, I was praying for him and his family as I drove along. A storm was brewing, and the sky was filled with clouds.

In the distance were the Blue Ridge Mountains. The wind was blowing hard, but just above me was an opening in the clouds. It seemed as if I could see through the gaping hole into the throne room of God. As I stared at the glorious skies, the Lord seemed to be reassuring me that while storms come and go, He is in control and that all things work together for good for those who love Him and are called according to his purposes (Romans 8:28).

When I arrived at the hospital, I was relieved to learn that Ron was doing better and was thrilled when several days later he took his first walk down the hall, a sure sign that the Lord had answered our prayers.

Five months passed, and we received a phone call that Ron was back in the ER and was being admitted, this time for pneumonia. Things were not going well. My son Joe, his wife Heather, and I set out for the same hospital, not knowing what we would find.

It was Palm Sunday and we had just celebrated communion at our church in preparation for the upcoming Easter Sunday services. Our spirits were both high and low. High, because we had commemorated Christ's death, burial, and resurrection and the assurance that faith in Him brings forgiveness of sin and eternal life. Low because Ron had been struggling for months with chemotherapy and radiation, and it seemed he would take one step forward and then fall back two. Today he had fallen back.

To my amazement, a glance into the heavens once again brought comfort and encouragement as I spotted a cross in the distance. It was as if the Holy Spirit was visually sharing with us that He is our Savior, the Divine Physician, the One who ultimately heals us of all diseases. Though we will have sickness and problems here in this world, He is our source of peace and joy amid the chaos. We can rejoice that one day we will pass through the portals of heaven and spend eternity with Him, free of pain and distress—whole again with new bodies exactly right for our new home!

A favorite psalm came to mind as we pulled into the parking lot:

"The heavens proclaim the glory of God. The skies display his craftsmanship.

Day after day they continue to speak;
night after night they make him known.
They speak without a sound or word;
their voice is never heard.
Yet their message has gone throughout the earth,
and their words to all the world." (Psalm 19:1-4)

After that glorious Sunday, Ron rallied and went home. Follow-up phone calls revealed he was his old self, full of good humor despite his situation. Only the Lord could provide such a positive attitude!

CHALLENGE: What about you? Does God speak to you in unusual, mysterious ways? If so, write about it in your journal, and share your experience, strength, and hope with others. If not, pray and ask Him to reveal Himself to you in his mysterious ways.

Holy God, Creator of the heavens and the earth and all that is within them, open our eyes to the wonders around us and make us keenly aware of the many diverse ways you speak to us.

Chapter Two

God Moments in Grief and Tragedy

"Even when I walk through the darkest valley, I will not be afraid for you are close beside me."
Psalm 23:4

From Tragedy to Triumph: When God Says "No"

"Then Jesus said, "Come to me, all of you who are weary and carry heavy burdens, and I will give you rest." (Matthew 11:28)

Fear almost paralyzed me as I responded to frantic cries from the back of the church, but adrenaline pumped through my system and propelled me out the back door and into the churchyard where my husband of 54 years lay gasping for breath. As I fell to the ground screaming and praying, I noticed his eye was swollen shut and turning black. He sounded as if he were gasping for his last breath. "Oh, God, spare him! Spare him! Oh, Honey! Don't die! Don't leave me!"

The ambulance arrived and we headed to the local hospital ten minutes away. A quick exam by the emergency room doctor determined he needed to be in a trauma hospital—38 miles away. As the sirens blared on the racing ambulance, my son Jon and I followed. The verdict: He had a brain bleed. The next few hours were critical.

As I sat in the waiting room while they hooked him up to monitors and IVs, I tried to piece together what had led up to this tragedy. For weeks Gerry had been having increasing difficulty walking. A neurologist had diagnosed him with possible hydrocephalus (fluid on the brain.) They had scheduled him for further tests in two weeks. Too late. Instead, he had staggered across the churchyard and plowed headfirst into the hardened earth.

For the next week, his situation was touch and go. Erratic heart rate, critically high blood pressure, no response or sign of consciousness.

People from many churches were praying for him. Suddenly, to our surprise, he opened his eyes one morning and asked for his breakfast. He had turned a corner. We were headed to rehab and three weeks later, home—to a new way of life filled with home health nurses, speech therapists, and physical therapists.

Even though I was delighted to be home, the situation was heartbreaking. My very bright, very competent husband could not walk unassisted and could barely feed himself. He could no longer add the simplest numbers or answer questions our young granddaughter could handle with ease.

The hydrocephalus could not be addressed until he more fully recovered. Weeks went by. Some days he seemed better—most days he did not. October 23 brought yet another tragedy. He was obviously worse, and a visit to the ER confirmed he was critically ill—possible perforated bowel. Emergency surgery revealed peritonitis, a serious infection in his abdomen. Thus, began weeks in the hospital.

Further complications. Gerry had been on home dialysis for kidney failure for over two years. The abdominal surgery would make it impossible to continue his home dialysis. He would need to be transported to a dialysis clinic three times a week, and he was not strong enough for the rigors of transport. He would have to remain hospitalized indefinitely.

My days were spent in the hospital trying to care for him. At night, I crashed at a nearby house for patient's families only to get up and head back to the hospital each morning. Thanksgiving and Christmas holidays came and went. The new year was approaching. The final bad news—a death sentence. Gerry could no longer continue his dialysis. It was too dangerous with his seriously high pulse and blood pressure issues. The decision: go home with Hospice care and make the most of the days he had left.

And so, we did. It was not what I wanted. It was not what I had prayed for at all. Hundreds of prayers on his behalf seemed unanswered.

And then my prayers changed. A sense of God's love and care took over my very being. Knowing that it was only days until the love of my life would leave me for his heavenly home, I began to pray for a peaceful passing.

Friends and family came and went. Gerry slipped into a coma; he seemed to be sleeping peacefully. As I waited, I took comfort in reading God's Word and books on heaven. Anne Graham Lotz' book, *Heaven, My Father's Home*, was particularly comforting. Even though I doubted that he could hear me, I read aloud to Gerry as well.

As I sat reading to him, his sister, Gail, slipped into his room to listen. I was struck by the appropriateness of a particular passage, "There will be no more hospitals, death, or funerals; walkers, canes of wheelchairs; ventilators, respirators or IVs. There will be no more Parkinson's disease, diabetes, or arthritis, cataracts or paralysis, MRIs or dialysis."

Gail sat down beside me as I continued to talk to him, "You know, Honey, one of these days, you will be greeted by a welcoming committee from heaven. I think your mother will lead the group."

Gail chimed in, "And just like she did when we were children, she will call 'Ger-ald' in her high pitched, shrill voice."

To our amazement, even though he had not responded or spoken in days, a series of three great big smiles lit up his face and he chuckled out loud! It seemed as if angels surrounded him! Then with the last chuckle, he was heaven bound!

I had prayed for a peaceful passing, and I was blessed by even more. I had prayed to be with him as he left this world for eternity. My prayers were answered. I believe I saw him smile one last time in this pain-filled world and that we watched him enter heaven's portals and experience the joy that will one day be ours.

The following months alone were difficult, but God was faithful. He carried me through the dark days and nights, and I rested in His peace that transcends all human understanding. I am confident of where my beloved lives today, and I look forward to joining him when Jesus calls me home. In the meantime, I cling to the Lord's promises:

"But those who trust in the Lord will find new strength.
They will soar high on wings like eagles.
They will run and not grow weary.
They will walk and not faint." (Isaiah 40:31)

"Jesus said, 'I am the resurrection and the life. Anyone who believes in me will live, even after dying.'" (John 11:25)

Challenge: Gerry knew Jesus as Lord and Savior. What about you? If you would like assurance that you will spend eternity in heaven, I encourage you to take these steps:

A – Admit you have sinned. (Romans 3:23)

B -Believe Jesus came to earth, was crucified, and was then resurrected as a sacrifice for your sins. (John 3:16)

C – Confess Christ publicly and commit your life to Him. (Romans 10:9-10)

Three easy steps. Then welcome to the family of God!

Precious Jesus, Savior and Lord, thank you for giving your life as a sacrifice for sinful men and women. Though we may not fully understand it all, we accept your gift of salvation by accepting your promise and committing our lives to you.

A Birthday Party in the Valley of Weeping

***"But those who trust in the Lord will find new strength. They will soar high on wings like eagles.* They will run and not grow weary. They will walk and not faint."**

Isaiah 40:31

The helium-filled balloons we were carrying down to our dock for release were shriveling—helium molecules become more compact and inactive when exposed to cold. The temperature was below freezing, the wind was blowing hard, and the lake was icing over. Yet our family, wrapped in warm coats, gloves, and scarves, had made our way carefully to one of my grandson Garrett's favorite places to send messages of love flying into the air. It was January 4, his 23rd birthday. He had died tragically six months earlier on June 25, 2017. This was his first birthday in heaven, and we were intent on celebrating it despite the weather.

Oddly, it seemed appropriate. Garrett loved the cold. We often spent a January weekend in the mountains so that he and his Uncle Joe could ski while the rest of us snow tubed.

As we huddled on the dock, balloons gripped in gloved hands, I couldn't wait to tell the assembled mourners of my encounter with the Still Small Voice that morning.

When I had sat down in the early morning hours to meditate and read the Word, I had prayed, "Oh, Lord, send us words of comfort. Carry us through this day. Let us experience your presence in miraculous ways." And he had answered—in amazing ways—and I was excited to share with them what He had said!

My first devotional book I read from that morning, I explained, was Sarah Young's *Jesus Calling,* and the related scripture was in Isaiah 40. What a blessing! Isaiah 40 is so beloved to me that its 31st verse is engraved on my husband's tombstone—which will one day be mine as well.

The day's focal passage, however, was on an earlier verse in the chapter which I read through chattering teeth:

"He tends his flock like a shepherd:
He gathers the lambs in his arms
and carries them close to his heart;
he gently leads those that have young." (Isaiah 40:11 NIV)

For the past six months the Good Shepherd had indeed carried us, his sheep, when we felt like fainting. He had comforted us and sustained us in numerous ways.

With as much excitement as I could muster in the frigid air, I shared with my near-frozen listeners that the second passage I had read from *Jesus Calling* was Psalm 139:

"I can never escape from your Spirit!
I can never get away from your presence!
If I go up to heaven, you are there;
if I go down to the grave, you are there.
If I ride the wings of the morning,
if I dwell by the farthest oceans,
even there your hand will guide me,
and your strength will support me." (Psalm 139:7-10)

What words of comfort! The Lord was here with us in this frigid place and in heaven with Garrett simultaneously!

Psalm 139 continues:

"You saw me before I was born.
Every day of my life was recorded in your book.
Every moment was laid out before a single day had passed.

How precious are your thoughts about me, O God.
They cannot be numbered! (Psalm 139:16-17)

Garrett's days, and our own, are in His hands! We can rest in the assurance that He is in control, He loves us, and He is with us here in this world and for eternity! We don't have to understand everything. We just need to trust Him.

Finally, I shared two passages for the day that had come from Sarah Young's *Jesus Always* that had touched my soul:

"Shout joyful praises to God, all the earth!
Sing about the glory of his name!
Tell the world how glorious he is.
Say to God, "How awesome are your deeds!"
(Psalm 66:1-3)

"...Go and celebrate with a feast of rich foods and sweet drinks and share gifts of food with people who have nothing prepared. This is a sacred day before our Lord. Don't be dejected and sad, for the joy of the Lord is your strength!" (Nehemiah 8:10)

My conclusions from my reading: Our God is awesome! His deeds are awesome! He amazes us every day with his miracles! He meets us where we are—when we are happy and when we are sad. He fills us with joy—even when are hearts are breaking! And yes, He wants us to celebrate! He wants us to enjoy the good gifts He has given us. He does not want us to be sad but to experience His joy—truly experience it!

With a mixture of sadness and joy, we let go of the balloons. In the frigid air, a few took off high into the sky. Others, though, were tempted to splash belly first into the water but gradually gained momentum and flew off. One seemed to get caught in the trees across the cove from us. We watched it with anticipation. Finally, it freed itself from the branches and flew away as well.

Like those balloons, we as a family are still struggling to fly; but in time, we are going to be o.k.—just fine! We might be stuck for a moment, but in time the wind—the Holy Spirit—will free us and we will take off, too!

As the birthday party moved from the dock to one of Garrett's favorite Mexican restaurants, our spirits lifted as we shared good food, humorous stories, and precious memories. We said good night and headed home.

I whispered a silent prayer of thanksgiving as I opened the front door into the house Garrett and I had shared. The Lord had carried our family through our first Thanksgiving, Christmas, and birthday without Garrett. We had survived, and the Lord was healing us moment by moment. Though some days, we may have trouble flying and sometimes we feel like splashing belly first into the abyss, we are beginning to gain momentum. Thank you, Jesus.

"What joy for those whose strength comes from the Lord,
who have set their minds on a pilgrimage...
When they walk through the Valley of Weeping
it will become a place of refreshing springs.
The autumn rains will clothe it with blessings." (Psalm 84:5-6NLT)

The Spirit is always at work! He's revving our engines, showing us His flight path, and preparing us for takeoff!

Challenge: What about you? Can you think of a time when the Spirit carried you through times of overwhelming grief? Write about it in your journal. List it in your Gratitude Journal. Share your testimony—your story—with someone who is struggling with grief.

Thank you, Lord, that you comfort us and carry us. May we remember your Word and carry out your commands: "All praise to God, the Father of our Lord Jesus Christ. God is our merciful Father and the source of all comfort. He comforts us in all our troubles so that we

can comfort others. When they are troubled, we will be able to give them the same comfort God has given us." (2 Cor. 1:3-4)

Tears in a Bottle

Precious in the sight of the Lord Is the death of His saints." (Psalm 116:15 NKJV)

My mother-in-law, Joyce Lancaster Luckadoo, was a simple woman. A devout Christian, her days were spent caring for family, ministering to loved ones who needed a helping hand, teaching children's Sunday School, and singing in the choir. Shortly before her death, she received a plaque for 50 years of Sunday School ministry, and she retired from the choir only when she could not walk up the three steps to the choir loft a few months before her passing!

Perhaps it was because of her faithfulness that the Lord sent a choir to sing their way through the halls of the Hospice House the morning she died. I can still hear "When the Roll Is Called Up Yonder I'll Be There" and other songs about heaven as I reflect on that morning.

Mama Joyce, as her grandchildren and great grandchildren called her, had grown up poor—the youngest of four girls. Her parents had worked in a cotton mill. They lived in a "company house" and made do with whatever they had. Three good dresses—that's all she had—two for school which she wore on alternate days and one for Sundays. A child of the depression, she was very frugal but also very generous in her own unique way.

She married at 18 and lived with one of her sisters when her new husband, Boyd, went off to war. She would bear his first child, Gerald, while he served in the Philippines, and she would single-parent her new baby until he was released from the military when Gerald was 2 ½ years old.

She would have a beloved daughter, Gail, about a year after his return. It was to this small family that she would devote her remaining years as wife and mother and then grandmother and great grandmother.

Though not a rich woman, she always had a gift for you whenever you visited—a piece of cake, a jar of pickles or green beans, a bag of frozen corn or something else she had preserved in her freezer.

Mama Joyce passed away on January 28, 2014. There are many bad jokes about mothers-in-law, but I was blessed. She was a wonderful mother-in-law! I miss her.

Several weeks after her passing, my husband, Gerald, his sister, Gail, and I began the difficult task of disposing of her possessions. An organized, tidy woman, Mama Joyce had accumulated little. She kept only the things that she truly treasured or used regularly. Having been a homemaker for 70 years, much of what she owned was worn out. Her motto, "Make do or do without," was obvious. She did, however, have two drawers in her dresser where she kept the things she really cared about—her treasures.

As I carefully removed the items in the "treasure drawers," I was drawn to an old pill bottle. When I opened it, I was surprised to find not pills but little baby's teeth. On further examination, I discovered the teeth had belonged to my husband Gerald. These "keepsakes" were a gentle reminder of how much she adored her son, the child she clung to in the long absence of his Daddy. The baby book accompanying the pill bottle detailed all his "firsts."

A moment of sadness overwhelmed me as I closed the book and gently placed it and the bottle in the moving box. Tears slipped down my cheeks. It felt like

I was somehow invading holy ground as I packed her "treasures" for removal.

In the moment's sadness, though, a reminder from Scripture brought comfort and joy.

"You keep track of all my sorrows.
You have collected all my tears in your bottle.
You have recorded each one in your book."
(Psalm 56:8)

How wonderful! Our Father—Abba—Daddy—has keepsakes from our lives. He keeps our tears in bottles as a reminder of how much He loves and cares for us. What comfort we can have in knowing that our doting Daddy loves us enough to minister to us when tears flow and hearts break.

After carefully closing the "Memories" box and gently placing it in the backseat of our SUV, I was overwhelmed by another word from Abba—a promise that He is there to comfort us now and forever!

"He will wipe every tear from their eyes, and there will be no more death or sorrow or crying or pain. All these things are gone forever." (Revelation 21:4)

What joy awaits us when we are united with Christ Jesus and reunited with dear ones who have gone ahead of us! I can almost hear the heavenly choir singing for us just as that church choir sang as Mama Joyce left us for heaven:

"When the trumpet of the Lord shall sound, and time shall be no more,
And the morning breaks, eternal, bright and fair

When the saved of earth shall gather on the other shore,
And the roll is called up yonder, I'll be there
When the roll, is called up yon-der,
When the roll, is called up yon-der,
When the roll, is called up yon-der,
When the roll is called up yonder I'll be there.*

CHALLENGE: What about you? Has the Lord blessed you with sweet memories of a dear loved one? Thank him and add to your gratitude journal. What about your own life? Are you living a life that will leave a legacy for your family? One rich in love, joy, peace—the fruit of the Spirit? If not, I encourage you to talk it over with your Creator and ask him what needs to change in your life—and then obey. You won't be sorry!

Loving Father, thank you for the saints you place in our lives to teach us by their examples how to live godly lives. Thank you that we can join them one day in our heavenly home.

*James Milton Black, 1893, public domain.

A Music Miracle

"The Lord your God is in your midst, The Mighty One, will save; He will rejoice over you with gladness, He will quiet you with His love, He will rejoice over you with singing." (Zephaniah 3:17 NKJV)
"God blesses those who mourn, for they will be comforted." (Matthew 5:4)

Sunday, September 9, my phone rang. It was one of those calls you hope you never receive.

Lee Morgan, a good friend, wept uncontrollably on the other end of the line as he asked, "Please pray for me! My daughter Erin died this morning. A tree fell on her house as she and her husband lay sleeping. We're on our way to Greensboro, but I needed someone to pray for us, and I thought of you!"

In shock and despair, we prayed together, and then he was gone. My heart ached for him and his family for I had recently lost a grandson in a sudden tragic accident. Nothing can prepare you for such gut-wrenching pain!

Fast forward seven weeks. It was Sunday, October 28, and I sat in my usual spot at Trading Ford Baptist Church.

I was pleased to see Lee and his wife Ginger sitting a few rows in front of me and made a mental note to speak to them as we left. The service began. The music soared. People rejoiced as hands waved in praise. Then the offertory began—an old hymn—*Be Thou My Vision*—one I did not remember having sung in years.

The song itself was out of the ordinary for our church. We usually sing more contemporary music. Yet the Lord was doing something unusual and important in the pew ahead of us, and the entire congregation was oblivious to it.

As if by divine appointment, Ginger exited the church at the same time I did. Lee had stopped to talk to my son Jon.

We greeted each other, and then she asked an odd, unexpected question. "Do you know how they pick the music for the service?" she asked.

Befuddled by her question, I responded, "Well, I assume our music director picks them. Why do you ask?'

With tears in her eyes, she said, "Well, they played that song "Be Thou My Vision" at Erin's funeral. I like the song and had wanted it played for her service, but I never told anyone except Lee. You can imagine our surprise when we got to the memorial service and it was one of the songs we sang. Today is Erin's birthday, and again I was surprised when we sang it. In fact, when I turned to Lee and looked at him, we just burst into tears."

"Wow," I commented. "Isn't it awesome when things like that happen! I just love those God moments. When they occur, you just know the Lord is showing up in a special way!"

As we left for our cars, I could not help but rejoice that the Lord was ministering to his children on a difficult day.

After Sunday lunch, I decided to learn more about Erin since I had never met her. I also wanted to know more about the hymn "Be Thou My Vision."

Erin, it seems, was an amazing young woman. According to her obituary, "Erin was a Greensboro native and Wolfpack graduate who was a vibrant woman and lover of life, and tirelessly gave of herself to make others' lives more whole. Whether she was hosting supper club or using her giftedness at United Way of Greater Greensboro, she gave to others wholeheartedly. Erin embodied such radiance and strength that she could give it away to others in abundance. Her endless supply of love and contagious joy left everyone feeling loved and unconditionally accepted. She was an active member of Christ United Methodist, and deeply committed to her relationships formed there."

One of the Lord's saints had gone home!

The history of the song "Be Thou My Vision" is amazing as well. Believed to be written in Ireland in the 8th century by a blind Irish monk, the hymn survived the centuries until Eleanor Hull translated the lyrics and paired them with a traditional Irish tune. Today the hymn has risen in popularity as contemporary artists have recorded it.

In retrospect, as Lee and Ginger tried to make sense of Erin's untimely death, they felt the Lord's presence through this hymn written hundreds of years ago, first at their daughter's funeral, and then again on her birthday. In so doing, they joined the multitude of Christians who have been comforted in miraculous ways through the Lord's divine intervention and His gift of music.

Regardless how He speaks to us, though, He gives us gentle reminders that He is our light both by day and by night. He is the source of our vision, our comfort, our wisdom, our inheritance, and our victory over the struggles of this life!

CHALLENGE: What about you? Has the Lord ever burst into your world and comforted you in some divine way so that you knew it was Him reaching out to you? Lee and Ginger felt his presence through song. You may have had other "God moments." If so, take a few moments to write about it in your journal and add it to your Gratitude List.

"For My thoughts *are* not your thoughts,
Nor *are* your ways My ways," says the Lord.
"For *as* the heavens are higher than the earth,
So are My ways higher than your ways,
And My thoughts than your thoughts." (Isaiah 55:8-9 NKJV)

Loving Father, thank you that you are the source of all comfort when we are overwhelmed with grief. Help us to allow you to hold us, to minister to us, and to reveal your purposes to us when we are in the pit of despair. Thank you for your love and compassion.

Welcome to the King's Haven

"Morning, noon, and night I cry out in my distress, and the* Lord *hears my voice." (Psalm 55:17)

Christmas Day, 2018, marked eighteen months since I came home to find that my precious 22-year old grandson Garrett had accidentally shot himself and lay dead in my basement. It was the most horrific day of my life. Nothing can fully explain the horror and agony of that tragic experience.

For months, thoughts of his lying there alone on the floor haunted me. I could not bear to go into the room. For a year I would awaken often to thoughts of his passing. The basement became an emotional tomb. Entering it was depressing, like going to a cemetery on the day of a funeral.

Already in great need of remodeling, the basement area became even dirtier and grimier since no one had the heart or the energy to clean it up. Garrett's shoes still lay on the hearth where he left them. His clothes were still strewn around. Items to be stored or discarded were piled high. The entire basement was frozen in a state of despair.

Finally, over a year after the tragedy, my eldest son, Jeff, said, "Mom, it's time to do something about the basement. It's not healthy emotionally. We as a family need to move on."

I knew he was right. It was time. I had prayed for months about what the Lord wanted me to do with the space. "How can we turn this place into a welcoming refuge instead of a mausoleum?" I asked. We needed a physical, and more importantly. a spiritual and emotional make over.

Everyone finally reluctantly agreed, and the months of remodeling began. Filthy carpets were ripped up. Ceilings were patched and painted. Worn out furniture was hauled to the dump. Loads of old items that basements accumulate were removed as well.

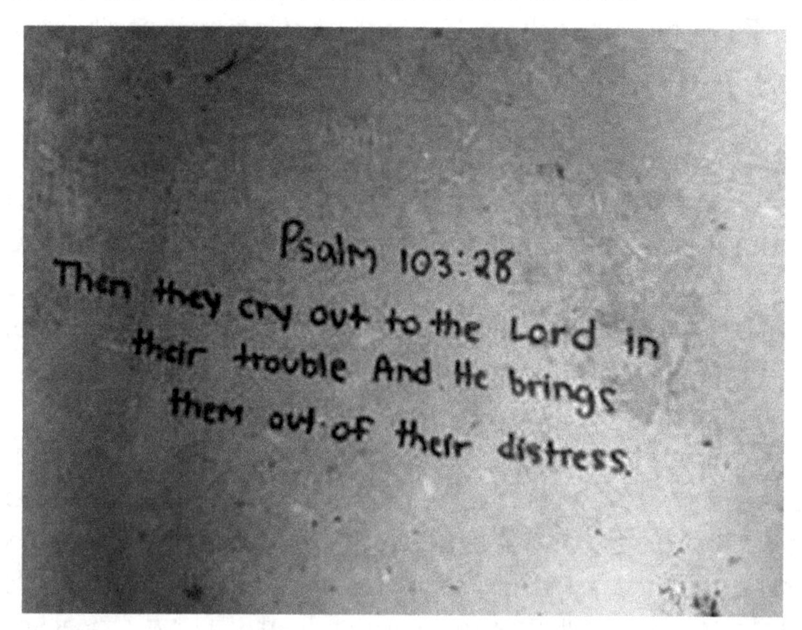

We searched for ways to draw closer to God and thereby bring peace and acceptance to our family as we worked. We prayed together often, and when the carpets were removed, we all wrote favorite Bible verses all over the floor before installing new floor covering. What a comfort! It was cathartic. Standing on God's Word became a physical reality!

The place became homier and more inviting. Even the smell improved—no more damp, moldy stench of old carpet.

Yet the memories of death persisted. Even though the place was physically more inviting, it was still cold to me.

It was Christmas Eve, 2018, now 18 months after Garrett's death. We had made many physical changes. We had prayed and prayed for peace. Yet there were still disturbing memories that filled my thoughts.

Then the Lord gave me a most wondrous Christmas present! As I sat doing my Bible study, I saw clearly a new vision. Though my grandson was lying on that cold floor, he was not alone as I had always imagined. Instead, the room was filled with angels. Two men were also there—Garrett's Papa Gerry, my deceased husband, and his Papa Sam, his grandfather on his mother's side. The room became not a cemetery but a launching pad for heaven! In my mind, it miraculously became the beautiful refuge I had wanted it to be!

Sitting there in awe, I remembered that the place even had a name! All the way back in 2007 on an early morning walk, the Lord had impressed on me that we needed to use our home as a refuge, a place of warmth and hospitality. As I had walked, I heard him give me the name—The King's Haven. I had not understood fully then what the Lord wanted me to do, and I had done nothing. Now it had become a reality!

My basement, my house, belongs to the Lord. It is to be a haven of peace and rest. No longer do I enter the basement and see where Garrett died as a dreadful place. Even in its disrepair, it was indeed a place of beauty as he was escorted into heaven by angels and his grandfathers! Garrett had literally left my house and moved into his heavenly home in the twinkling of an eye. One day I will see him. What a blessing! My mind and my thoughts had been transformed in a matter of moments. I was reminded of three of my favorite verses:

"And do not be conformed to this world, but be transformed by the renewing of your mind, that you may prove what is that good and acceptable and perfect will of God." (Romans 12:2 NKJV)

"Therefore, if anyone is in Christ, he is a new creation; old things have passed away; behold, all things have become new." (2 Corinthians 5:17 NKJV)

"That is what the Scriptures mean when they say, 'No eye has seen, no ear has heard, and no mind has imagined what God has prepared for those who love him.'" (1 Corinthians 2:9)

As our family gathered that year for our Christmas celebration, I shared with them my hopes for my home and its new name. Through tears of joy, we prayerfully dedicated The King's Haven to the glory of God as we also remembered Garrett and Papa Gerry.

Welcome to The King's Haven!

CHALLENGE: What about you? Has the Lord ever changed your thinking and thereby helped you deal with pain and loss? If so, praise Him and write Him a love letter, poem, or song. Pray for someone you know who may need a word of comfort and encouragement during difficult days and share your experience, strength, and hope.

Source of All Comfort, renew our minds and help us to see You and your purposes as we cope with the difficulties and losses of life and seek to minister to others who are hurting.

Miracle Man

"For God loved the world so much that he gave his only Son so that anyone who believes in him shall not perish but have eternal life." (John 3:16 TLB)

His doctor called him "miracle man" because he had survived stage 4 lung cancer and countless other health issues longer than any patient he had ever treated. In my eyes, he was a "miracle man" as well.

Always the optimist, he never lost his sense of humor during his many-year battle with heart issues, neuropathy, losing a leg to diabetes, and finally lung cancer that sapped him of his strength and his appetite. His real name was Ron, and he was my dear brother. Though I was 18 months older than he was, he always called me "Little Sister" because he was 6'2", 275 pounds, and I was much smaller than he was until the cancer robbed him of 125 pounds.

My last visit with Ron was on June 21, 2018. Bedridden, unable to feed himself, barely able to sit up when physically lifted by others and placed in his wheelchair, he was still optimistic and still searching for hope.

It took my son Jon to lift his lanky frame from the bed, his wife Merry Lynn to drag along the oxygen tank, and me to open doors and help maneuver him to the car so we could drive him to the doctor's office. When we finally arrived, we had to take the foot pedals off the wheelchair to make room for Jon to lift him out of the car. Then Jon pushed the wheelchair while I carried his feet and Merry Lynn rolled the oxygen.

In retrospect we were an amusing entourage. If not for the severity of the situation, I'm sure we looked ridiculous! The office staff laughed in amusement as we tried and tried to put the foot pedals back on the wheelchair. No success. The nurse came to escort us into the examination room. She carried feet, Merry Lynn brought the oxygen, and I pushed the wheelchair.

Now assembled, we tried to explain to the doctor our challenges with transporting Ron. Jon made the comment that it would have been much easier if Ron had just relaxed and bear-hugged him tighter. Ron, who sat silently, seemingly disengaged, slowly raised his head and quipped, "Well, I just didn't want to get my nose any further up your armpit or I could have done better!"

The room erupted in laughter. Ron was famous for his one liners, and a good laugh relieved some of the tension in an otherwise difficult day. King Solomon knew as much when he penned his famous proverb, "A cheerful heart is good medicine, but a broken spirit saps a person's strength." (Proverbs 17:22)

Dr. Rees, a wonderful oncologist who is ever the encourager and the optimist, prescribed a new experimental drug—one that has had a 70 percent success rate in reducing tumors and with few side effects. He commented as we prepared to leave that if the drug were successful, we would all see a "real miracle." Hope resonated in his encouraging words.

Hope—that's what we all wanted. Ron asked me three times to tell him what the doctor had said during his visit. Every time a big smile spread across his haggard face as he said, "That's encouraging, isn't it?"

Ron the "miracle man," was ever hopeful; however, he was able to take only a few doses of the "miracle drug" before he met real Hope face to face.

According to Merry Lynn, Ron awoke early on the morning of June 29. He ate a few bites of breakfast. Then he cheerfully welcomed Misty, his home health aide, when she came to help with his bath. Misty was concerned that his blood pressure was too low and suggested calling the doctor. With his usual upbeat manner, though, he quipped to her and Merry Lynn that "he had a good feeling" about the day.

Recognizing that the low blood pressure was a warning signal, Merry Lynn asked him, "If you were to go to heaven today, would you prefer to go from home or from the hospital?" His response? "I want to stay right here in my bed where I can see my birds." Ron loved nature and the outdoors and had several bird feeders outside his window.

Later in the day, he asked Merry Lynn to sit with him as they shared a hamburger for lunch. Needing to put some gardening tools in the garage, Merry Lynn walked outside for a few short minutes. To her surprise and dismay, Ron was unresponsive when she returned. He had slipped away to his new "home" to meet Jesus, the real Miracle Man, and beloved family and friends who had gone ahead of him.

In a discussion about heaven and dying a few weeks earlier, Ron told me that he always assumed he would just go to sleep when he died—and he did! He just fell asleep very peacefully and woke up in heaven.

When I learned of his passing, I was reminded of a dream—or a vision—I had had a few weeks earlier. In the vision Ron was with my dear husband, Gerry, and my precious grandson, Garrett, who both moved to heaven within the previous two years. Both Gerry and Garrett were laughing as they stood arm in arm watching Ron dance a jig.

Ron was whole again—youthful, smiling from ear to ear, white teeth glistening, blue eyes twinkling. He was clad in a crisp blue shirt and khaki shorts, no longer missing the leg he'd lost to diabetes. He no longer needed a cane or a walker, and he was dancing!

Ecclesiastes 3:1, 2, 4 tells us:

"For everything there is a season, a time for every activity under heaven. A time to be born and a time to die. A time to cry and a time to laugh. A time to grieve and a time to dance."

For Ron, his time to die had passed. It was now a time of laughter and dancing—no more crying, no more pain, no more medicine and no more wheelchairs.

Isaiah 25:8 assures us that "He will swallow up death forever! The Sovereign Lord will wipe away all tears."

Ron had experienced the ultimate healing! Ron met the REAL MIRACLE MAN, Jesus Christ, and he had found the ultimate Hope—one not found in any pill, drug, or surgery.

Death brings sorrow for those left behind but great joy for the ones leaving if they know Jesus as Lord and Savior. Ron did!

"So now there is no condemnation for those who belong to Christ Jesus. And because you belong to him, the power of the life-giving Spirit has freed you from the power of sin that leads to death," Romans 8:1-2

CHALLENGE: If you died today, are you sure you would go to heaven? If not, I'd encourage you to follow what some call the "Roman Road," a series of scripture passages that explain the way to salvation. You'll be glad you did! Your life here will never be the same as you enjoy the abundant life (John 10:10). In His time, you, too, may dance your way into the presence of the Miracle Man, Jesus Christ!

- "For everyone has sinned; we all fall short of God's glorious standard." (Romans 3:23)

- "The Scriptures tell us, "No one is acceptable to God!" (Romans 3:10 CEV)
- "When people sin, they earn what sin pays—death. But God gives his people a gift—eternal life in Christ Jesus our Lord." (Romans 6:23 ERV)
- "God has shown us how much he loves us—it was while we were still sinners that Christ died for us!" (Romans 5:8 GNT)
- "If you declare with your mouth, 'Jesus is Lord,' and believe in your heart that God raised him from the dead, you will be saved. For it is with your heart that you believe and are justified, and it is with your mouth that you profess your faith and are saved." (Romans 10:9-10 NIV).
- "Everyone who calls on the name of the Lord will be saved." (Romans 10:13)

Jesus, our Savior, thank you for giving your life so that we can live eternally with you by simple faith. Draw us to you and prepare us for our new life in heaven, whenever you call us home.

The Battle Is Over!

But thanks be to God, who gives us the victory through our Lord Jesus Christ. (1 Corinthians 15:57 NKJV)

It was over! The battle with lung cancer gone wild was over! My dear sister-in-law, Gail Luckadoo Dobbins, had a new home. She had left behind her worn out "tent" and taken up residence in a mansion in heaven.

Family and friends celebrated her life and home-going Friday, January 11, 2019, at Trinity Baptist Church, Mooresboro, North Carolina. She, however, had left us and moved "home" on the previous Tuesday when pneumonia finally took the remaining breath from this saint.

It was my pleasure to have been Gail's sister-in-law since October 15, 1961, when I married her brother Gerald. More than a relative by marriage, though, she was the sister I never had, a dear friend and confidante. I loved her easy-going ways, her sweet disposition, and her quirky sense of humor. She could get tickled over little things.

Once in the early years of my marriage, I missed a step leaving her house and fell sprawling. After she found out I was not hurt, she burst into laughter. Years later when she was trying to help her mother Joyce out of the car and into the house, they lost their balance and fell in the yard. As she lay pinned to the ground with Mom on top of her, they could not get up for laughing. Gail loved slapstick!

I spent my last days with her watching *My 600 Pound Life*, *Pimple Popper*, and *Say Yes to the Dress*—TV shows that she loved. Even though I'm not a fan, I enjoyed just spending time with her. Our bond grew even stronger as we shared snacks and sodas and laughed out loud.

I will miss her sweet ways, her compassion, and her encouragement—even when she was the one who needed encouraging. I will miss our late-night phone conversations when neither of us could sleep—chatting about anything and everything—and nothing.

Gail faced many struggles in her life, but she was not a whiner nor a complainer. Though she would never have seen herself in such a way, I saw her as the biblical character Deborah, the fearless leader of her little family who never gave up. Faced with many tragedies—the loss of her only son Jason in an automobile accident; the loss of her father Boyd to a stroke; the many years of care giving for her mother Joyce before her death; the death of her husband Dean from lung cancer; the extended illness and death of her only brother Gerald; the tragic death of her nephew Garrett, and ultimately her own bout with lung cancer which had metastasized to her bones and other parts of her body, she remained strong.

She adored her only grandson Andy, his wife Keelee, and great-grandchildren, Paislee and Peyton. She was still babysitting the kids up until a week before her death.

Ever a prayer warrior, she spent time every day interceding for others and reading her well-worn Bible and her favorite devotional books, *Jesus Calling* and *Jesus Always*. As 2019 dawned, she was excited to begin reading through a new chronological Bible since her old one was falling apart. I think you can learn much about a person by checking out the condition of her Bible.

Facing surgery for throat cancer on January 2, 2019, she wrote in the margin of *Jesus Always* the night before:

"My Lord and my Joy will walk with me tomorrow. Thank you, Jesus."

Little did she know that this would be her last entry, for the battle was almost over. Her favorite passage from John 14 was soon to be a reality:

"Let not your heart be troubled; you believe in God, believe also in Me. In My Father's house are many mansions; if it were not so, I would have told you. I go to prepare a place for you. And if I go and prepare a place for you, I will come again and receive you to Myself...I am leaving you with a gift—peace of mind and heart. And the peace I give is a gift the world cannot give. So don't be troubled or afraid." (John 14:1-3, 27 NKJV)

Praise God, the victory was won! As Paul wrote, "Then when our dying bodies have been transformed into bodies that will never die, this Scripture will be fulfilled: 'Death is swallowed up in victory. O death, where is your victory? O death, where is your sting?'" (1 Corinthians 15:54-55)

What a victory! What a party! I can just imagine the reunion that took place in heaven!

Yes, that Tuesday was a time of death, of crying and grieving here on this earth. In the heavenly realms, though, I believe that afternoon was just the beginning of a joyful celebration! There was a family reunion beyond family reunions taking place! Lots of heavenly food. Lots of laughter. Lots of talking. Gail was at last reunited with Jason, Dean, and all her dear family who had already moved to heaven. I believe they gathered on Tuesday afternoon to welcome her home. I can see them in my mind all waiting together on the mansion's porch ready to celebrate Gail's arrival. Wow, what a party!

Goodbye, dear Sister! I will miss you, but I am glad that the battle is over! One day perhaps we'll sit in heaven's rockers and enjoy a late-night chat once again. After all, we'll have all eternity to catch up!

CHALLENGE: What about you? Lost a dear friend or loved one recently? Still grieving for him or her? If so, why not thank the Lord for the memories and share them with other friends and family. In Paul's words, "May God our Father and the Lord Jesus Christ give you grace and peace." (Romans 1:7)

Thank you, Breath of Heaven, that you comfort us in times of grief and then enable us to comfort others in their times of need.

Breaking Out of a Chrysalis

"He will once again fill your mouth with laughter and your lips with shouts of joy." (Job 8:21)

It had been only a week since the funeral for Aunt Gail, my sister-in-law and dear aunt to my children, when our family headed off to White Oak Lodge Resort in Gatlinburg for our annual winter trip to the mountains. Returning to Gatlinburg had been a difficult decision. We had not been there since the losses of my husband Gerald in 2016 and grandson Garrett in 2017. They were such an integral part of our trips to this location that returning there was difficult emotionally.

Gatlinburg, I might add, was Aunt Gail's favorite vacation spot. She and her family visited there almost every year.

When we sat down to watch television on our first night there, my youngest son, Joe, was scrolling the TV guide. He spoke up, "Let's watch *Dr. Pimple Popper* in memory of Gail." He remembered that I had said it was one of her favorite shows. I smiled to myself. I had spent several hours watching the show with her and knew what to expect.

As they settled in to watch the show, I grabbed my phone, eager to take pictures, for I knew how squeamish most of my family is.

The first case involved the removal a cyst on a woman's head. It was just behind her ear, and it was HUGE—the size of a baseball or even a softball. Sure enough, they reacted just as I expected. As Dr. Pimple Popper removed the large mass, the facial expressions told it all!

Shock, surprise, amazement, and disbelief overwhelmed son Joe and his wife Heather.

Laughter, on the other hand, overtook daughter-in-law Kandee, a nurse, and granddaughter Kaity. Aunt Gail would react similarly, I thought to myself, if she could see their antics from heaven. She loved a good belly laugh!

Scripture came to mind as I reflected on the evening: "He will once again fill your mouth with laughter and your lips with shouts of joy." (Job 8:21)

A growing awareness came that perhaps it is better to acknowledge our losses, share our feelings, do something in memory of our dear ones, and even have a good laugh or two.

Knowing Gail, I am certain she would agree. After all, she is enjoying the grandeur of heaven while we watch cysts being removed on a reality TV show. She would find that hilarious!

As our week progressed, we chose to re-visit attractions that the entire family had once enjoyed. We visited two places with bittersweet family memories--Cooter's, an indoor bumper car racetrack, and the chairlift in downtown Gatlinburg.

While memories shrouded in grief briefly crowded into the present, we had a wonderful time racing those cars at Cooter's and riding up the mountain on the chairlift bundled up like mummies in the frigid air.

Even though we did not set out on this trip to deal with our grief, we did. One choice after another, we moved ahead one more step toward acceptance and healing.

I recently read a wonderful meditation in *Daily Guideposts* by Sabra Ciancanelli in which she compared grief to a chrysalis that we wear for a long time until it eventually changes us forever and brings us to a place of ascension.

As a family, we have not yet ascended, but we are making progress. Praise God, he directs our steps each day to bring us closer to full acceptance and peace.

The words of Solomon in the book of Wisdom are ever so true, "Everything seems to go wrong when you feel weak and depressed. But when you choose to be cheerful, every day will bring you more and more joy and fullness." (Proverbs 15:15 TPT)

CHALLENGE: How about you? Have you found that confronting your fears and making new memories have helped you deal with your grief? If so, share your pictures and memories with others. If not, spend some time asking the Lord to help you see the past in a new light filled with wonderful moments that can bring comfort even amid the pain.

God of All Comfort, thank you for bringing us joy and peace amid profound grief and for orchestrating moments of laughter that soothe our weary souls.

Fishing in Heaven

"He reveals deep and mysterious things and knows what lies hidden in darkness, though he is surrounded by light." (Daniel 2:22)

February 16. What a relief. Valentine's Day and its festivities were over for another year.

It had been two years since Gerry, my husband, had died, and only a few months since my 22-year-old grandson, Garrett, who lived with me, passed away in a tragic shooting accident. My house was empty except for my cat and me. Holidays—even insignificant ones like Valentine's Day—were difficult.

I paused for a moment and realized it was a gorgeous day. The weather was unseasonably warm; and as I looked out on High Rock Lake, I thanked the Lord for its beauty and for the blessings of the many years we had lived there. I never tired of the spectacular view from my sunporch—the lake, the small island in the distance, the many birds, even a fish jumping into the air from time to time. It was a magical place filled with precious memories of family times—fishing, boating, tubing, and water skiing.

Sitting down at the kitchen table with a cup of coffee and my Bible, I opened *Daily Guideposts*, a devotional book I've enjoyed for years. Searching for the day's meditation, my eyes were drawn to the caption, "I will fully satisfy the needs of those who are weary and fully refresh the souls of those who are faint." (Jeremiah 31:25 NET)

How appropriate! That was me. Weary and faint.

I picked up my Bible and read the related scripture from Psalm 127.

The verses were familiar. I read on, "Children born to a young man are like arrows in a warrior's hands. How joyful is the man whose quiver is full of them!" (Psalm 127:4)

I recognized it as one of Gerry's favorite passages. He often quoted it when he shared his testimony, and I had read it at his funeral. His three sons and five grandchildren—all his family—were precious to him.

"I miss him, Lord, but thank you that he has Garrett with him in heaven," I prayed. "I wonder what they are doing today. I'll bet they are fishing, whatever that looks like there! I wish I could fish with them again. It's so lonely here, Lord. Help me understand what I'm to do with myself!"

Papa Gerry and Garrett together in heaven "fishing." That was a comforting thought—one I needed to record in my journal.

My mind drifted to happier days; and as I wrote, I remembered one day when Garrett was about three years old. He, Papa Gerry, and I were out fishing on a similarly beautiful day. Quite unexpectedly, Garrett picked up his Papa's new fishing rod and dropped it overboard. Even though the water was very cold, Papa Gerry quickly jumped in after it.

Struggling to operate the trolling motor, I maneuvered the boat over to where he stood in waist deep water, and he crawled back into the boat. Though he did not think it was funny as he sat shivering and bedraggled, I could not help but laugh, and the story became a precious memory over the years as it was told and retold.

Memories. That's what I had. As I plunged back into reality, I cried out, "Lord, what now? It seems like all I have is memories. What shall I do with myself until I join Gerry and Garrett in heaven? How do I manage this grief and depression?"

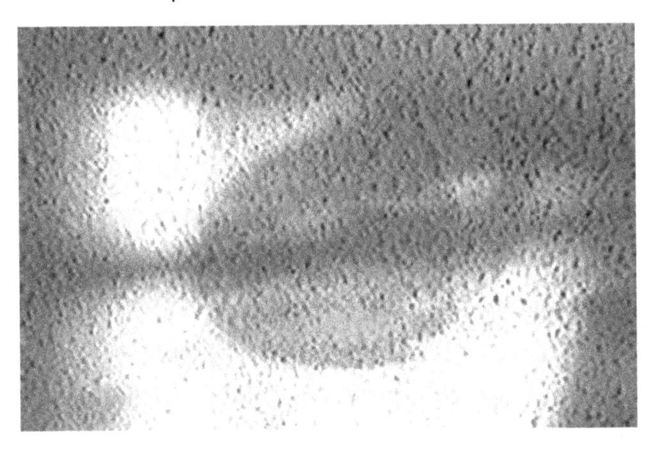

Wallowing in self-pity and reminiscing over days gone by, my attention was suddenly drawn away from my writing to a strange glimmer on the ceiling just over my head—colors—beautiful shimmering colors. Blue, orange, pink, and yellow against a brilliant white light. What was that unexplained light? Where was it coming from? I had sat in that same spot every day for years, but I had never seen it.

I put down my pen and stood up to find the source of the glowing image. As I wandered across the room, I discovered that the sun was streaming through a stained-glass sun catcher in my dining-room window and reflecting on the ceiling. Odd—since my back porch blocks the sun from ever reaching that window. In all the years we had lived in the house, I had never seen sun directly in my dining room!

On closer examination, I studied for the first time the vibrant colored scene in the sun catcher flooded with light. It was of beautiful boats—red, orange, pink, yellow—sailing on a gorgeous sea of blues and greens against a sky filled with fluffy white clouds. It was breathtaking—reminiscent of beautiful days we had shared on our lake. I grabbed my phone and took pictures.

To my surprise, the background of the picture showing lovely High Rock Lake was grey—drab—almost colorless.

"How could this be?" I asked myself as I studied the photograph. "How could our beautiful lake look so blah?"

Then quietly, the Lord seemed to answer, "Your earthly lake, with all its beauty, is but a dim copy of my heavenly lakes. One day you'll join Gerry and Garrett for another fishing trip. For now, stop fretting and carry out my purposes there."

"What purposes, Lord?" I prayed. "What am I supposed to do without them?" And I heard his Still Small Voice reminding me of a familiar verse, "Come, follow me," he said, "and I'll show you how to fish for people." (Matthew 4:19 CEB)

And then He seemed to take me back to the day years ago when I sat on a mountaintop overlooking a stream and accepted his call to ministry. I had heard him clearly say, "So go and make followers of all people in the world...Teach them to obey everything that I have told you to do. You can be sure that I will be with you always." (Matthew 28:19-20 ERV)

As I closed my journal, I reached for my "To Do" list. It was time to move on. It was time to accept my situation. It was time to get out my "fishing pole" again and start fishing.

CHALLENGE: What about you? Has the Lord ever spoken to you in a mysterious way that jolted you out of a pit of depression? Write about it in your journal and add it to your gratitude list. Invite someone to go "fishing" with you or share the gospel with someone who is lost in a sea of despair.

Oh, God of Miracles. Thank you for sending us messages of comfort and direction in ways beyond explanation. Help us to recognize and obey.

Chapter Three

God Moments in Addiction and Recovery

"I will exalt you, LORD, for you rescued me. You refuse to let my enemies triumph over me. O LORD my God, I cried to you for help and you restored my health. You brought me up from the grave, O LORD. You kept me from falling into the pit of death."

Psalm 30:1-3

Choices Have Consequences

"A prudent person foresees danger and takes precautions. The simpleton goes blindly on and suffers the consequences." (Proverbs 22:3)

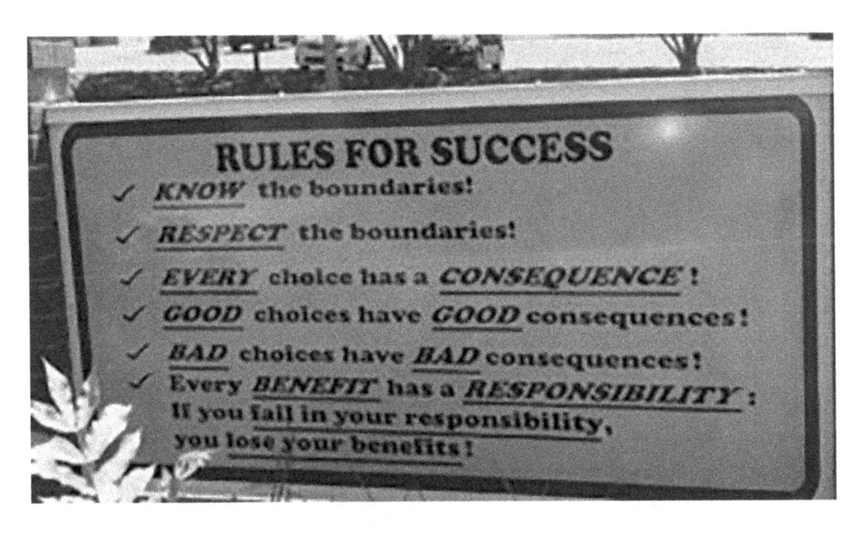

The sign at Capstone Recovery Center reads in part, "Good choices have good consequences. Bad choices have bad consequences." Oh, how true!

My cat, Puddy Tat, and I learned this lesson the hard way! Each morning he enjoys a short jaunt outside since he spends most of his time within the confines of my house. One morning he did not return from his walk. It was after dark when he showed up at my back door—bedraggled and dragging his tail behind him.

Something was wrong with him, but he hissed if anyone tried to check him out.

Guesses as to his problem included snake bite, a UTI, and a broken tail. To my surprise, though, a trip to the vet revealed he had been in a fight, and he needed surgery for an abscess. After an overnight stay in the hospital and a bill for $401, he returned home with a collar to keep him from trying to remove the drain lines from his incision on his backside. He was not a happy boy.

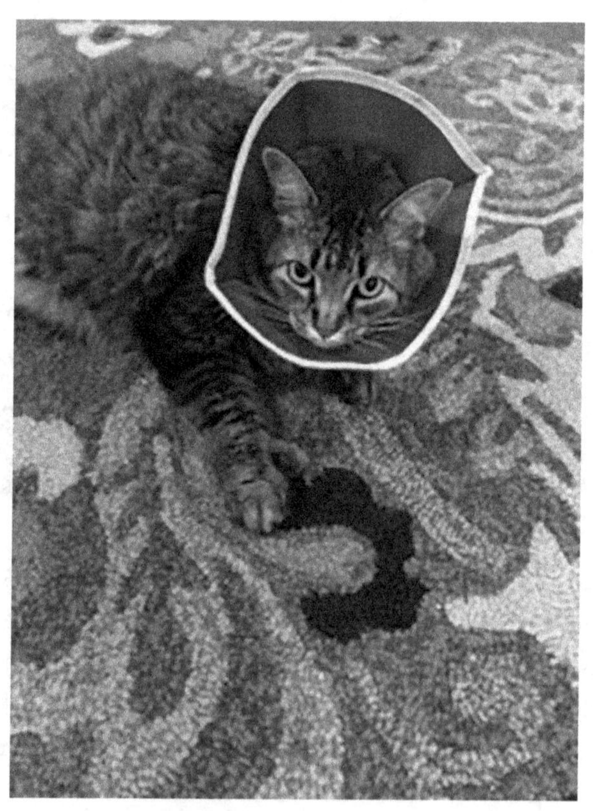

As I reflected on his situation, I remembered the sign at Capstone where I volunteer each week. Our bad choices frequently do have bad consequences, and they did for us on that fateful morning.

I then remembered a large yellow feral cat that lives in a pipe under our road—probably the other fighter—and wondered about his welfare. Since Puddy is an 18-pound Maine Coon with seven claws on one front foot and six on the other, I can't help but imagine what his opponent must have looked like following their wrestling match. Though I haven't seen him since the encounter, he is still around, for Puddy frequently sits at the front window looking longingly at the outdoors. He doesn't know it, but it will be some time—if ever—before he goes back outside for a possible follow-up bout.

One of the earliest shows I ever watched on television was *Truth or Consequences*. When contestants could not quickly answer a silly trivia question, they paid the consequences by having to take part in an embarrassing stunt of some sort. It was always hilarious for the audience—but humiliating for the participant. That's how Puddy looks now. Cute and funny to the observer but not pleasant for the cat who finds eating a challenge and grooming himself impossible!

Bob Barker, the host of the show, would sign off with "Hoping all your consequences are happy ones."

Sadly, we know that is impossible!

As if orchestrated from above just for me and my situation, Pastor Mike Motley's sermon at Trading Ford Baptist Church the Sunday following our trip to the vet was on choices.

His text was from Deuteronomy 30:19-20:

"Today I have given you the choice between life and death, between blessings and curses. Now I call on heaven and earth to witness the choice you make. Oh, that you would choose life, so that you and your descendants might live! You can make this choice by loving the Lord your God, obeying him, and committing yourself firmly to him. This is the key to your life. And if you love and obey the Lord, you will live long in the land the Lord swore to give your ancestors."

I found several key points in the message thought provoking:

- God has a plan and purpose for our future, but He has given us free will. We can choose whether to follow His plan or our own.
- Small choices can have a big impact on our lives and our futures. Even seemingly insignificant decisions can have huge consequences.
- Our choices affect people other than ourselves. Friends and family also suffer when we make bad choices.
- We should make choices with the intended outcome in mind.

Sadly, the children of Israel in the Old Testament made bad choices often—and suffered bad consequences. So did my old cat. So do all human beings.

While it is accurate that bad things happen to us sometimes because of the bad choices of others rather than ourselves, we need to think before we act so that we can ensure the best possible outcomes in choices that are within our control.

The Lord has reassured us in his Word that he wants the best for us. And what is our part? To choose wisely!

"'For I know the plans I have for you,' says the Lord. 'They are plans for good and not for disaster, to give you a future and a hope.'" (Jeremiah 29:11)

Challenge: What about you? Made any bad choices that resulted in bad consequences? The good news is that it's not too late. Choose life!

Wise Counselor, may we indeed obey your Word as we make choices each day: "Commit your actions to the Lord, and your plans will succeed." (Proverbs 16:3 NLT)

PS Capstone Recovery Center is a transition house for women struggling with addiction. As one of the volunteers there each week, we strive to help the residents realize that while their bad choices did have bad consequences, there is hope for recovery through Jesus Christ. To watch lives transformed and families restored is a blessing beyond description. "For with God nothing shall be impossible!" (Luke 1:37)

If you or someone you know needs such assistance, check out the website at www.capstonerecoverycenter.org and contact Miriam Ramirez, the executive director.

Just Who Is Family?

"As Jesus was speaking to the crowd, his mother and brothers stood outside, asking to speak to him. Someone told Jesus, 'Your mother and your brothers are standing outside, and they want to speak to you.'

Jesus asked, 'Who is my mother? Who are my brothers?' Then he pointed to his disciples and said, 'Look, these are my mother and brothers. Anyone who does the will of my Father in heaven is my brother and sister and mother!'" (Matthew 12:46-50)

Jesus had much to say about "family," and some of it seemed harsh! To be honest, I could never comprehend until recently why Jesus made some of the statements he made.

Some time ago, I was talking with several women who were recovering from addiction. Most of them were sad as the Christmas season was approaching and they would not be spending time with their biological families because those families were not "safe." If there is ongoing substance or physical abuse, anger issues, and dysfunction at home, then that makes it unwise to spend time there. Hearts were very heavy as we discussed options. Loneliness pervaded the room even though there were several of us gathered together.

It reminded me of Jesus' words:

"I have come to set a man against his father, a daughter against her mother, and a daughter-in-law against her mother-in-law." (Matthew 10:35)

Wow! Shocking words, it would seem, until we remember that followers of Jesus are to love Him above all others. Further, believers are not always welcome in their own families. The last Beatitude Jesus gave us in the Sermon on the Mount which is also the last principle in Celebrate Recovery states:

"God blesses those who are persecuted for doing right, for the Kingdom of Heaven is theirs. God blesses you when people mock you and persecute you and lie about you and say all sorts of evil things against you because you are my followers. Be happy about it! Be very glad! For a great reward awaits you in heaven. And remember, the ancient prophets were persecuted in the same way." (Matthew 5:10-12)

I can remember times in the distant past of great loneliness during holiday seasons even though I had my biological family around me. Sadly, there were even times when I dreaded such occasions and couldn't wait for them to be over because someone was always drunk or angry or arguing before the day ended. As I listened to the young women share their fears and anxieties, I knew what they were talking about!

Yet, I also know that the Lord is faithful! He provided "family" through his church during those difficult days—His "forever family." He answered prayers for family restoration, and in time, He even used my Christian witness to bring lost family members to Him—what a blessing! Though these experiences were difficult and often painful, in the end they brought glory to God! James was right when he wrote,

"Dear brothers and sisters, when troubles of any kind come your way, consider it an opportunity for great joy. For you know that when your faith is tested, your endurance has a chance to grow. So, let it grow, for when your endurance is fully developed, you will be perfect and complete, needing nothing." (James 1:2-4)

In retrospect, I can see clearly what Jesus meant in His encounter with His biological family. It wasn't that He didn't love them; rather it was that He knew situations sometimes arise when the body of Christ becomes much more important than our kin. Loyalty to Him is more important than loyalty to people on earth:

"If you love your father or mother more than you love me, you are not worthy of being mine; or if you love your son or daughter more than me, you are not worthy of being mine." (Matthew 10:37)

What, then, can one do when biological family is not "safe" either emotionally, physically, or spiritually? Here are a few suggestions:

- Pray without ceasing for your family and for yourself.
- Love and communicate from a distance.
- Set healthy boundaries. (If you don't know how to do this, check out the book *Boundaries: When to Say Yes, How to Say No to Take*

Control of Your Life by Henry Cloud and John Townsend.**)**

- Cultivate relationships with Christian brothers and sisters.
- Become involved in a church family.
- Join a Celebrate Recovery group. (You can find a national listing of sites at www.celebra-terecovery.com)
- Volunteer at homeless shelters, nursing homes, or other ministries.
- Reach out to others who are also lonely.
- Ask the Lord to help you find your ministry and serve others.

But what if you don't yet know Jesus as Lord and Savior? What if you're not sure you are a part of the family of God? Then it's as simple as ABC to become an adopted child of the Most High King. Just pray to him as you take these steps:

A – Admit that you're a sinner. "For everyone has sinned; we all fall short of God's glorious standard." (Romans 3:23)

B – Believe that Jesus is God's son and that he loved you enough to pay the penalty for your sins by dying on the cross.

"But God showed his great love for us by sending Christ to die for us while we were still sinners. And since we have been made right in God's sight by the blood of Christ, he will certainly save us from God's condemnation." (Romans 5:8-9)

C – Confess your sins, ask Jesus into your heart, and commit your life to Him.

"If you openly declare that Jesus is Lord and believe in your heart that God raised him from the dead, you will be saved. For it is by believing in your heart that you are made right with God, and it is by openly declaring your faith that you are saved." (Romans 10:9-10)

That's it! If you sincerely followed the ABC's and committed yourself to Christ through prayer, welcome to your new "forever family" of God, my new sister or brother!

"For the wages of sin is death, but the gift of God is eternal life through Christ Jesus our Lord." (Romans 6:23 NLT)

Hallelujah!

CHALLENGE: What about you? Ever struggled with dysfunction in your biological family to the extent that the environment was not safe for you? Why not follow the ABC's and join a loving new family—the eternal family of the Lord Jesus Christ?

If you've already made the choice to follow Christ and join his forever family, share your testimony with someone who needs to hear it and help them find love, peace, and joy through Jesus Christ.

Loving Father, we thank you for adopting us into your family through our faith in Jesus Christ, our Savior, and providing us a home in eternity with you and fellow believers.

Choose Life!

"Your eyes saw my substance, being yet unformed. And in Your book, they all were written, the days fashioned for me, when as yet there were none of them. How precious also are Your thoughts to me, O God! How great is the sum of them!" (Psalm 139:16-17 NKJV)

Chrystina—follower of Christ—was radiant as she stood before family and friends gathered to celebrate her graduation from Capstone Recovery Center. She had reason to beam. She had successfully completed seven months in recovery from drug addiction—seven months in which she had not only laid down her addiction but more importantly had come face to face with who she was in the past, who she is now in Jesus Christ, and who she wants to become in the future as she follows her Lord. She was victorious—and it showed on her face.

It had been my privilege to watch her grow from a timid, scared young woman into a leader and a woman of prayer. As chair of the board at Capstone and a volunteer in the ministry, I had served as her mentor as we read through the full New Testament, worked through the biblical *12 Steps to Conquering Chemical Dependency*, studied Henry Blackaby's *Experiencing God*, and discussed Rick Warren's *What on Earth Am I Here For.* (By the way, she had completed more than 15 Bible studies with other volunteers during her time at Capstone! Participants are immersed in the Word!)

I had also had the privilege of watching her live out her faith as she volunteered each week to help me prepare a supper for approximately 50 people who attend our Celebrate Recovery ministry at Trading Ford Baptist Church every Tuesday.

A growing prayer warrior, she volunteered to begin an intercessory prayer ministry for Celebrate Recovery and then asked Pastor Mike Motley if she could lead a similar ministry for our church. The Lord was using her in a mighty way. It was amazing to watch how the Great Physician was healing and remolding her!

After she received her certificate of completion from Dr. Oscar Ramirez, director of counseling at Capstone, and her "crown" reflecting her status as a daughter of the King of the Universe from Miriam Ramirez, executive director, it was my turn to ask her two questions.

"Chrystina, what is your mission statement? What is your purpose in life?" I asked.

Through tears of joy and with a smile on her face, she quoted Deuteronomy 30:19-20.

"I call heaven and earth as witnesses today against you, that I have set before you life and death, blessing and cursing; therefore choose life, that both you and your descendants may live; that you may love the Lord your God, that you may obey His voice, and that you may cling to Him, for He is your life and the length of your days." (Deuteronomy 30:19-20 NKJV)

Her mission? I choose life! I will love the Lord, obey Him, and commit myself to Him.

Oh, that we would all share that mission statement!

I then asked her about her ministry plans. (All graduates of Capstone are encouraged to minister to others for it is in giving of ourselves that we get out of the selfishness that dominates us.)

Her plans: to continue the Celebrate Recovery prayer ministry she had begun and to become a part of the Celebrate Recovery children's ministry.

Wow! With her newly found faith walk, a love for God's Word, and a commitment to ministry, Chrystina has what she needs to live the abundant life promised by King Jesus.

"The thief (Satan) comes only in order to steal and kill and destroy. I (Jesus) came that they may have and enjoy life, and have it in abundance [to the full, till it overflows]. (John 10:10 AMP)

As I reflect now on Chrystina's graduation and her commitments to the Lord, I am reminded that the Lord is transforming her into an "oak of righteousness." He promises in his word:

"To all who mourn in Israel, he will give a crown of beauty for ashes, a joyous blessing instead of mourning, festive praise instead of despair. In their righteousness, they will be like great oaks of righteousness that the LORD has planted for his own glory." (Isaiah 61:2-3 NLT.)

My prayer for Chrystina is that she will continue to grow in her faith and develop such strong roots in Christ that she will never again be blown over by Satan or her own selfish desires—that she will be an "oak of righteousness."

Challenge: What about you? Have you wrestled with the Lord and determined your mission statement? If so, you are aware that it simplifies life. It will define your ministries and keep you from wasting precious time. If not, I would encourage you to seek the Lord's guidance as you write down both your mission statement and your ministry calling. Life is short. Our days are numbered. Why not spend time on things of eternal value!

Dear Savior and Redeemer, thank you that you created us to be your children and your heirs. May we listen and fulfill your purposes and your call on our lives.

Drinking Deadly Water

"With joy you will drink deeply from the fountain of salvation! In that wonderful day you will sing: 'Thank the Lord! Praise his name! Tell the nations what he has done. Let them know how mighty he is!'" (Isaiah 12:3-4 NLT)

One of my favorite trees is dead. I will miss it! For the past 24 years—ever since I moved in my house—it has been a source of shade as we sat by our swimming pool on hot summer days. No longer will we be able to find respite from the hot sun on scorching afternoons.

Why, I asked myself, would it die? While it is a mature tree, it doesn't appear to be that old. Its roots are near High Rock Lake, so it didn't succumb to drought. In fact, to look at it, you would think it's alive. It still has a few scattered leaves, but the tree expert says it is dead. It will not bear green leaves ever again. Even though there is no apparent reason for it to die, it is dead.

On further reflection, though, it dawned on me. The tree also sits on the drain line for our pool. All summer long when we backwash the pool, we dump chlorinated water on its roots. A check of the Internet says too much chlorine will kill plants. We have apparently inadvertently killed it!

Sadly, this reminds me of what we do as we search for peace, love, and joy in all the wrong places. We thirst for something deep within ourselves that is missing. We try to satisfy that thirst with alcohol, drugs, sex, relationships, money, possessions, stuff—all poor substitutes for the real "Living Water." As a result, we slowly die—we kill not only our physical bodies but also our spiritual ones.

Just like my tree, we shorten our lives trying to satisfy an unquenchable thirst that is, in fact, not physical but spiritual.

Jesus met just such a woman at a well in Samaria. She had tried to satisfy her spiritual thirst through relationships with men. Having, had five husbands, she was living with a man who was not her spouse.

Jesus offered her "Living Water," and when she accepted it, He changed her life. So excited was she that she took off to the town where she was no doubt an outcast and shared about her experiences with Jesus. Her bold testimony led others to run to Him, and they, too, were saved. (John 4:1-15)

Dr. R. C. Sproul, American pastor and theologian, once described the unbeliever as lying "flat dead drowned" on the bottom of a swimming pool just like the one in the shadow of my dead tree. He is dead in his sins. He can't possibly save himself. Then the Lord—the Lifesaver—reaches down and pulls the dead man out of the water and breathes life back into his dead spiritual body. The man, once resuscitated, recognizes his Savior and clings to Him with thankfulness and joy.

Many of us are in a frantic search for the solution to our spiritual thirst problem. We try anything and everything the world offers with no relief. We want peace, but we end up stressed out, frazzled, worried, and anything but peaceful seeking peace in all the wrong places.

When we finally reach "bottom" and realize that we are drowning, may we cry out with the psalmist:

"O God, you are my God;
I earnestly search for you.
My soul thirsts for you;
my whole body longs for you
in this parched and weary land
where there is no water." (Psalm 63:1)

Further, may we cling to Jesus' assuring promise:

"To all who are thirsty I will give freely from the springs of the water of life." (Revelation 21:6)

Finally, may we remember the words of Jeremiah, "But blessed are those who trust in the Lord and have made the Lord their hope and confidence. They are like trees planted along a riverbank, with roots that reach deep into the water. Such trees are not bothered by the heat or worried by long months of drought. Their leaves stay green, and they never stop producing fruit." (Jeremiah 17:7-8)

Jesus is offering each of us "Living Water." May we, like the woman at the well, answer,

"Please, sir," the woman said, "give me this water! Then I'll never be thirsty again." (John 4:15 NLT)

Challenge: What about you? Are you drinking from the world's polluted water or have you found the Source of Living Water? If you are drowning in pollution, why not accept the gift of Living Water and turn your life over to Him. You will not regret it! If you know the Source, I pray you drink deeply from His fountain and satisfy your thirsty soul. Spend some time writing in your Gratitude Journal. Share the Source with those who are dying without hope.

Precious Jesus, may we turn to you and accept your gift of Living Water—your eternal salvation—while leaving behind the poisoned waters of this world that cannot satisfy. May we drink from your well like a dying man drinking from a firehose. Fill us, Lord. Fill us!

Love Affair with the King

"Jesus replied...And you must love the Lord your God with all your heart, all your soul, all your mind, and all your strength.'" (Mark 12:30)

Her face was animated; her eyes glistened with tears; her voice was passionate. The woman sitting across the table from me at a Celebrate Recovery meeting—I'll call her Meagan—was sharing about her new love. "I can't stop thinking about Him. People are probably tired of listening to me, but I can't stop talking about Him either!" If you overheard the conversation without knowing the circumstances, you would have thought that Meagan was talking about a new boyfriend or her fiancé; but instead, she was sharing about the newfound love of her life, King Jesus.

She reminded me in many ways of another young woman—I'll call her Joy—I had heard share at a Capstone Recovery Center small group meeting a few weeks earlier. "I just can't get enough of reading the Bible. I go to sleep reading it. I want to know everything about Him. He has transformed my life!" Adoration, passion, and gratitude seemed to exude from Joy's inner being. A "baby" Christian, she was "in love" with her new "husband"—King Jesus—whom she had met only a few months before.

As the ministry director of Celebrate Recovery at Trading Ford Baptist Church and a teacher at Capstone Recovery Center, I hear these testimonies often. New Christians who have met Jesus in recovery from addiction are often exuberant. You can spot them in a worship service. They are often the ones with hands raised and tears flowing who sing with such passion that you can't help but notice them, even though they are oblivious to those around them.

I sometimes wonder why many of us who have been Christians most of our lives lack the zeal and enthusiasm of these babes in Christ. Perhaps we have allowed ourselves to become lukewarm rather than on fire—a condition Christ warned the church at Laodicea about: "I know all the things you do, that you are neither hot nor cold. I wish that you were one or the other! But since you are like lukewarm water, neither hot nor cold, I will spit you out of my mouth! You say, 'I am rich. I have everything I want. I don't need a thing!' And you don't realize that you are wretched and miserable and poor and blind and naked." (Rev. 3:15-17 NLT)

As we take a hard look at our own love affair with King Jesus, I think it appropriate to take our spiritual temperatures to see whether we are hot or cold or just lukewarm. Are we so fervently in love with Him that we want to talk about Him all the time? Do we love Him so much that we want to immerse ourselves in His love letter to us—the Holy Bible? Or are we merely going through the motions, wearing a mask, pretending to be pious but rotting away inside?

One of the most overlooked characters in the Scriptures is the prophet Anna. An 84-year-old widow whose husband had died after only seven years of marriage, Anna chose to spend all her time in the Temple worshiping God with fasting and prayer. Then one day she had the privilege of meeting Jesus, and her life changed!

"She (Anna) came along just as Simeon was talking with Mary and Joseph, and she began praising God. She talked about the child to everyone who had been waiting expectantly for God to rescue Jerusalem." (Luke 2:36-38)

Anna shared her testimony with anyone who would listen.

Two other people I admire in the Scriptures who couldn't stop talking about Jesus were Mary Magdalene and the demon-possessed man whom Jesus healed.

In Luke 8:1-3 we learn that Jesus cast seven demons out of Mary and that she, along with several other women, traveled with the apostles and used her resources to support Jesus' ministry. Later we find her at the foot of the cross and then at the empty tomb. Because of her faithful love and obedience, Mary was commissioned by Jesus as the first missionary when He sent her to share the good news of His resurrection with the disciples. (John 20:14-18)

Then there's the demon possessed man who was running wildly through the tombstones—naked and out of his mind. Jesus healed him of his demons and restored him to sanity. The man was so grateful to Jesus that he wanted to follow him. "But Jesus said, 'No, go home to your family, and tell them everything the Lord has done for you and how merciful he has been.' So the man started off to visit the Ten Towns of that region and began to proclaim the great things Jesus had done for him; and everyone was amazed at what he told them." (Mark 5:19-20)

What about us? What is our "spiritual temperature?" I've been wrestling with this question for several weeks, and during that time two quite different songs from vastly different eras have inspired and challenged me in my quest.

First, contemporary Christian singer, Zach Williams, invites us to Dr. Jesus in his song "Chain Breaker." Right in the middle of the song, Williams challenges those of us who are healed to share the Good News of our healing. "If you believe it and receive it. then testify," he sings.

Testify! That's what we should be doing! Testifying!

Second, "Go Tell it on the Mountain," one of my favorite Christmas songs, also challenges us to testify. Though dating to the Civil War era, it was first published in 1907 by John Wesley Work, Jr., director of the Fisk University Jubilee Singers as a part of his book, *New Jubilee Songs as Sung by the Fisk Jubilee Singers*. Tradition reports that early on Christmas morning, long before sunrise, Fisk students would walk through the buildings singing this awesome song:

"Go, tell it on the mountain,
Over the hills and everywhere.
Go, tell it on the mountain,
That Jesus Christ is born!"

May we as Christ followers be as excited to share the gospel as Meagan, Joy, Anna, Mary Magdalene, the demoniac, Zach Williams, and John Wesley Work, Jr. May we be willing to "Testify, testify," with all the enthusiasm we can muster! May there be no doubt in the minds of those around us that we are passionately in love with the Christ, the Son of the Living God—King Jesus.

Challenge: What about you? How is your love affair with the King of the world? Want to testify? Write your own testimony in your journal. Add every new blessing that comes to mind to your Gratitude list. Seek out at least one person today with whom you can share your testimony—and do it!

Savior of the World, open our eyes to opportunities to share the gospel, and then give us courage to share YOU and your gift of salvation with those who need to hear the Good News.

Chapter Four

God Moments in Times of Spiritual Growth and Spiritual Warfare

"I pray that from his glorious, unlimited resources he will empower you with inner strength through his Spirit. Then Christ will make his home in your hearts as you trust in him. Your roots will grow down into God's love and keep you strong." (Ephesians 3:16-17)

I Thought I Saw a Puddy Tat!

"If you make the* Lord *your refuge, if you make the Most High your shelter, no evil will conquer you; no plague will come near your home. For he will order his angels to protect you wherever you go."
(Psalm 91:9-11)

There he sat, crouched amid the plants on my sunporch, waiting for some unwitting bird who would come for breakfast at the birdfeeder outside the window over his head. I could not help but smile in amusement. He—my very own Puddy Tat—lives up to his namesake. He loves to sit in wait of his "Tweety Bird" so he can jump up and try to grab him, failing to realize there is a barrier separating them.

You may remember the cartoon characters Tweety Bird and Sylvester. Poor Sylvester never had a chance. Tweety Bird always outwitted him. It was almost as if he had a special sense that protected him. "I think I see a Puddy Tat," he would often say. If those birds outside my window could talk, I'll bet they would say the same thing!

Images from 1 Peter 5:8 spring to mind as I watch him:

"Be alert and of sober mind. Your enemy the devil prowls around like a roaring lion looking for someone to devour." (1 Peter 5:8)

Fortunately for the Christian, we have an invisible barrier protecting us just like that window protects the unsuspecting bird from the claws of my big fat cat, but our barrier has a name. His name is Jesus—the one who died for us and provides a barrier for us from the evil one.

Now, Puddy Tat is not a bad cat. He just does what cats do—chase birds and other critters. For the poor bird, though, it would be devastating if he could reach him.

Satan and his demons, on the other hand, are evil. According to the Scriptures, "The thief (Satan) does not come except to steal, and to kill, and to destroy. I (Jesus) have come that they may have life, and that they may have *it* more abundantly." (John 10:10 NKJV)

It is important for us to remember that while Satan cannot take the souls of believers, he can torment us and keep us from enjoying the abundant life Jesus promised. The solution to our dilemma when Satan rears his ugly head? Run to the Savior! Tweety Bird had Granny who looked after him. We have a Savior waiting to protect us! The Scriptures tell us what to do.

"The Lord is like a strong tower. Those who do what is right can run to him for safety." (Proverbs 18:7 ICB)

Flee—run—don't dally! Those birds sitting on my bird feeder do not linger when my cat hits the window. No, they fly away fast! That's what we must do. When we come face to face with evil, we need to run.

Several years ago, my husband Gerry and I were with a group of youth at a rally, and the speaker spoke on this passage. I will never forget his illustration. As he stood on the stage six feet above the auditorium's floor, he said he would show what it meant to flee. He suddenly jumped off the stage and raced down the center aisle and out the back door. The speed with which he ran was incredible. It was as if the Savior stood outside the door and he wanted to fly into his arms of protection as quickly as possible. That's what we must do when Satan comes visiting—run to the Savior who waits for us with open arms!

And what about unbelievers who do not yet have a Savior?

The Word gives them a way to Divine protection, "If you openly declare that Jesus is Lord and believe in your heart that God raised him from the dead, you will be saved." (Romans 10:9)

The bottom line? For believers, the source of protection from Satan and his minions is Jesus Christ. Thank God we have a barrier to protect us! May we never forget there is freedom in Jesus Christ!

Challenge: What about you? Ever experienced protection from the Evil One? If so, meditate on the circumstances, write about it in your journal, and thank Him for His care. If not, consider giving your life to Christ and accept His protection.

Mighty God, Savior, thank you that you protect us from Satan and watch over us even when we are oblivious and unaware. May we never take your protection for granted.

A Hard Lesson in Humility

"Pride ends in humiliation, while humility brings honor."
(Proverbs 29:23)

I know I have arrived at old age. My sons are now parenting me—and I don't particularly like it!

Over and over, son Jon has warned me about wearing flip-flops and open-toed bedroom slippers. Over and over, son Joe has warned me about being careful navigating my basement stairs. Over and over, son Jeff has had to come and care for me when I have injured myself. Over and over, I have chosen to do as I pleased—continuing to wear what I want to wear and do what I wanted to do.

My lack of humility finally caught up with me.

The plastic boxes containing Christmas decorations needed to be moved to the basement. No one had been by the house to help me. "I can move them myself," I said, as I took the first one. Trying to avoid carrying it down the stairs since carrying heavy items is against the "rules," I decided to pull them down as I headed down backward. Bad choice! Wearing my favorite loose slippers, I tripped and fell the last three steps and landed hard on my behind scattering Christmas decorations helter-skelter.

Terror filled my heart! I had just been released from my doctor who performed back surgery in September with a warning that I had further degeneration in my lower spine and that I should be careful. "What have I done in my haste?" I asked myself.

I immediately texted son Joe who lives nearby: "Come and get me up!" As I sat there crying, I thought about that poor woman in the commercial who calls, "Help me! I've fallen and I can't get up!" That was me!

As Joe and his wife Heather arrived and gently helped me to stand, I was aware of pain in my left hip, left hand, and left ankle. No lower back pain—yet. Then began the ice—Joe's remedy. The Arnica—daughter-in-law Stephanie's remedy. The Aleve—Heather's remedy. Woe is me! I am old!

A family prayer request went out from my phone, "Please pray! I've fallen!"

Fortunately, they were right. The prayer and the remedies worked. No lasting damage. Praise the Lord!

As I sat down the next morning and read the meditation from "*Fixing My Eyes on Jesus*" by Anne Graham Lotz, I was convicted! "Be Humble" was the title. She wrote:

"Peter was unwilling to humble himself and allow Jesus to do something for him (see John 13:3-6)...His attitude was typical of you and me. It can be a serious wound to our pride to be served. Whose offer of help are you refusing for prideful reasons? Are you refusing to even admit you need any help at all...God clearly commands us in Scripture to 'humble yourselves (see

James 4:10, 1 Peter 5:6) Be obedient to His command. Express your obedience in a willingness to be served.""

Now that hit me right where it hurts! I was further reminded in Proverbs 16:18:

"Pride goes before destruction, And a haughty spirit before a fall." (Proverbs 16:18 NKJV)

That was me! Prideful and haughty! I've learned my lesson! No more flip flops and no more stair climbing loaded with boxes!

Woe is me! My sons have become my daddy!

On the other hand, being served may be o.k. I'll just sit back and let them wait on me. After all, I waited on them for a long time! LOL

CHALLENGE: What about you? Ever suffered bad consequences because of pride? Spend some time today confessing pride to the Lord and making amends to those you may have harmed because of prideful ways. Remember, though, that even though we may be getting older and need some help along the way, the Lord isn't through with us yet! There's still work to do; and He has promised to take care of us, sometimes through the helping hands of others!

Loving God, forgive my prideful, impatient ways and help me walk in humility on this path you have set before me. Help me to remember your Word and claim its promises:

"I will be your God throughout your lifetime—until your hair is white with age. I made you, and I will care for you. I will carry you along and save you." (Isaiah 46:4)

*Anne Graham Lotz. ***Fixing My Eyes on Jesus***. (Grand Rapids Michigan: Zondervan, 2018.), p. 26.

Transforming a Cast Sheep into a Bell Sheep

"So Jesus told them this story: "If a man has a hundred sheep and one of them gets lost, what will he do? Won't he leave the ninety-nine others in the wilderness and go to search for the one that is lost until he finds it? And when he has found it, he will joyfully carry it home on his shoulders. When he arrives, he will call together his friends and neighbors, saying, 'Rejoice with me because I have found my lost sheep.' In the same way, there is more joy in heaven over one lost sinner who repents and returns to God than over ninety-nine others who are righteous and haven't strayed away!" (Luke 15:3-7)

Several years ago, I was given a figurine of Jesus holding an adoring lamb with two other sheep playing at his feet. It has become a treasured possession. It reminds me of myself and of Psalm 23, a favorite scripture passage.

I like to tease my grandchildren that I am the one in His arms. They assume, I suppose, that I think I'm special—that I think He loves me most. That is not the case at all. Rather, I see myself as the wayward one, the one who kept needing special attention because I had gotten myself lost or into trouble.

Perhaps you have heard it said that in ancient times a shepherd would sometimes break the leg of a wayward lamb to keep it from wandering away or leading the other sheep into harm's way. He would then bandage the leg and carry the injured lamb on his shoulders until the leg healed. By that time, the lamb would become so attached to the shepherd that she would no longer wander but would stay close to her caregiver.

After much research, I cannot verify that this is a fact. The truth is that many of us are like wayward sheep; and we end up breaking our own legs, making it necessary for the Shepherd to search for us, bind up our wounds, carry us, and restore us. We chase after the things of this world that appear wonderful, and then we find ourselves attacked by Satan, eating slop in a pig pen like the prodigal son (Luke 15:11-32), or falling into a slimy pit of despair. In other words, many of us are prone to go our own way, while others of us are just downright rebellious.

As for me, I can be a wanderer, and that is the real reason I see myself as the one in Jesus' arms. As a child, I was timid and just wanted some measure of stability in my life. When I grew up and could make my own choices, I turned into a control freak who wanted her own way and desired to control not only myself, but also those closest to me.

An insecure people pleaser, I had an "ought to" list that dominated my life. I found it hard to say "no" and often overextended myself. What resulted was a person with too much to do and too many commitments.

I also tried to live with one foot in the world and one in the church. I served the Lord out of a sense of duty. I wanted all that this world offered and my place in God's kingdom, too. It did not work! What Jesus said was true, "No one can serve two masters; for either he will hate the one and love the other, or he will be devoted to the one and despise the other. You cannot serve God and mammon [money, possessions, fame, status, or whatever is valued more than the Lord]. (Matthew 6:24 AMP)

Over time, I developed many "idols" in my life—possessions, prestige, house, cars, work, clothes, and even alcohol to relieve the stress and strain. Instead of having the happiness that this world promises, I ended up anxious, overworked, and stressed out. I was anything but peaceful, joyful, and happy.

My life was falling apart, I couldn't sleep, I was having panic attacks, my marriage was in jeopardy. Finally, after a particularly horrendous night, I surrendered. Like a cast sheep—one that is on its back and can't get back up—I was totally exhausted. I lay on my back begging and pleading for the Good Shepherd to rescue me and give me a fresh start. Thankfully, He heard my plea and granted me a new beginning.

While He was carrying me close to his heart, I finally learned what it meant to live in a love relationship with Him. I no longer wanted to serve Him out of duty but out of love. He carried me for a long time until I learned to be more obedient and to stay close to Him. Then He put me down and taught me to walk beside Him. Finally, one day, to my utter amazement, He hung a bell around my neck, and asked me to call other wayward sheep to Him. I was now a bell sheep!

My walk with Him has not been perfect. Living in this world is hard. Satan is always out to get us. I have had to deal with problems, heartache, disappointments, the loss of loved ones, and sickness just like everyone else. But during those hard times, my communion with the Good Shepherd has grown sweeter and sweeter. He has continued to pick me up and carry me when I could not carry myself. After each crisis, He has comforted me until I was strong enough for Him to put me down and let me walk again. The things of this world have continued to fade as my attention to the Shepherd has continued to grow.

Challenge: Perhaps you've become a cast sheep. Perhaps you've been the wayward one, gotten yourself into lots of trouble, wandered off, or fallen in the slimy pit. Perhaps you've tried to do it all and found that you are tired, stressed out, joyless, unhappy, and miserable. Perhaps you're the one the Good Shepherd is calling. If so, I encourage you to give up and answer Him. Allow Him to rescue you, comfort you, and nurture you. Allow Him to carry you. And then, in time, let Him put you back down to walk close to His side, eventually ringing the bell to call other lost sheep to Him. What an honor to be a bell sheep calling, "This way to Jesus!"

He is waiting and ready to welcome you with open arms. Come!

Loving Abba, thank you that you come looking for us when we wander and that you rescue us from our waywardness. May we stay close to you and become your bell sheep, calling others to you.

Overcoming Fear: Crossing the Royal Gorge

"I prayed to the Lord, and he answered me. He freed me from all my fears." (Psalm 34:4 NLT)

"Do the thing we fear, and death of fear is certain." — *Ralph Waldo Emerson*

For years, I struggled with a fear of heights. I can remember a visit to the Empire State Building as a young woman and being terrified to go near the windows. I even had nightmares as a child about being driven in a car off a high bridge into a river.

It seems I am not alone. According to several recent studies, fear of heights and fear of flying are both in people's top five fears along with a fear of public speaking, which was also a real problem for me as a young adult.

Recognizing that a fear of flying was a serious handicap in our modern world, I asked the Lord for help; He resolved that fear years ago when I climbed on a plane and flew to Seoul, Korea, where my husband

Gerry was stationed. The fear of heights, however, had been harder to conquer. On our family vacation to Breckenridge, Colorado, though, I had a real opportunity to deal with this fear once again.

To prepare for our trip, I selected a Bible study for us to share during our family devotions time. We always spend part of our time on vacation wrestling with some theological or moral issue. This year, the Lord directed me to *Soul Detox: Clean Living in a Contaminated World* by Craig Groeschel. Though I had never heard of the book or the author, I was mysteriously drawn to it; and it turned out to be an excellent Bible study for us.

In his book, Groeschel discusses how we are being corrupted by the world through lethal language, radioactive relationships, false beliefs, cultural toxins, and—**fear**!

On Tuesday, our focus turned to Chapter 2, "Unlocking the Chokehold of Fear." As a part of the discussion, I shared that a former colleague of mine, Jim Gentry, used to quote Dale Carnegie when we would co-teach leadership classes.

"Do the thing you fear to do and keep on doing it… that is the quickest and surest way ever yet discovered to conquer fear."— *Dale Carnegie*

Carnegie was right. Until we learn that we can do what we fear, we will be kept in bondage unable to live the abundant life the Lord has in mind for us.

With our discussion of fear fresh in our minds, we headed out on Thursday to the Royal Gorge Bridge. Though we did not yet know it, we were getting ready to apply what we had learned. Famous as the highest suspension bridge in the United States and among the top ten highest bridges in the world, the Royal Gorge Bridge attraction also includes the Cloudscraper Zip line, the Royal Rush Skycoaster, and the Aerial Gondolas—all over 1000 feet in the air above the Arkansas River!

Now you may think you don't have to zipline across the Royal Gorge to overcome your fears, and that's true. The Lord, though, puts challenges in our paths; and until we overcome them, we may be unable to do what he wants us to do. I love the Nike slogan "Just Do It"—and we did!

We walked across the bridge, and we rode the Aerial Gondolas. Some of us ziplined; and others even rode the Skycoaster! Whew! Scary, exhilarating, perhaps not the first thing one does when dealing with a fear of heights, but we did it—and we have pictures and t-shirts to prove it! I was proud of my fellow adventurers. I knew it took God and guts to "just do it!"

Two of my favorite Bible verses on the subject of fear are 2 Timothy 1:7: "For God has not given us a spirit of fear and timidity, but of power, love, and self-discipline," and Psalm 34:4: "I prayed to the Lord, and he answered me. He freed me from all my fears."

CHALLENGE: What about you? Is fear paralyzing you? If so, why not give it to the Lord completely, and ask Him to help you overcome it. Then, just do it! Afterward, write about it in your journal, and spend some time meditating on fear in his Word.

Father God, our Creator and Protector, help us to give our fears to you and to say with the psalmist: "I prayed to the Lord, and he answered me. He freed me from all my fears." (Psalm 34:4)

In Search of Pure, Living Water

"As the deer longs for streams of water, so I long for you, O God." (Psalm 42:1 NLT)

I took a shower last night for the first time in several days. It was such a blessing!

My well has been on the blink, and it has taken Son Joe and his able assistants Sons Jon and Jeff a long time to figure out what was wrong with it. It turned out I had a busted pipe under the ground. It was hard to find and hard to fix in the cold and rain.

In the meantime, I had a valuable lesson in what our great grandparents must have endured in the days before indoor plumbing! Did you know that you can take a bath with a pitcher of water and a bowl? Did you know that you can wash dishes with two small pots of water? Did you know that it is a big job to carry water to flush a toilet, bathe, or wash dishes? (Well, at least I have a toilet inside—and not an outhouse—ugh!)

We Americans are spoiled! I hear about the desperate need for pure water in some countries in the world, and I have a better appreciation of their plight. My pump which was working at 25 percent capacity would pump water into my house, but it was red muddy. The thought of drinking it, washing clothes in it, or even bathing in it was not a pleasant one.

Since I live on High Rock Lake, Joe has suggested that I may be drinking lake water. That is a most unpleasant thought since the water is full of mud and other pollutants from heavy rains!

Again, how did our ancestors ever survive before they had time to dig clean wells or go to the store and buy some Aquafina or Dasani or install a whole-house water filter? Little wonder diseases such as cholera were common and would devastate families and communities.

Many people like myself use bottled water all the time for drinking because they need assurance of a safe water supply or because they just like the taste or convenience of water in a bottle. Sadly, I read that there are companies in the world selling counterfeit bottled water! Rather than filling the bottles with mineral water, the bottlers are filling them with water straight from the tap!

As I stood in my shower basking in the flow of clean warm water last night, I could not help but think of the parallel to clean spiritual water. Jesus met a woman at a well in Samaria and asked her for a drink. (John 4:1-42) She reluctantly supplied it. Because of her encounter with Jesus, she received a priceless gift—Living Water! Pure Living Water! It quenched a much more important thirst than her physical need—a spiritual need that transcends this world into eternity.

Jesus even called himself the source of Living Water. "Anyone who believes in me may come and drink! For the Scriptures declare, 'Rivers of **living water** will flow from his heart.'" (John 7:38)

When I think of Living Water and its power, I don't think of the dribble from a faucet or even the pulsing water from a shower. Rather, I see with my mind's eye the mighty magnificent Niagara River flowing with great, rumbling force over Niagara Falls—a wonder to behold!

Having experienced "Living Water," I know it to be an overwhelming, mighty, powerful force that transforms lives for all eternity! It floods not just the physical body but the spiritual body!

Are you enjoying "Living Water" or settling for the world's counterfeit polluted puddles? Just like fake bottled water, the world is full of fake "spiritual water" that the hucksters claim will bring great health and happiness. Sadly, the promises of the world are empty, for Satan and the world offer "dead" not Living Water.

If you are spiritually thirsty, I have good news! Jesus will satisfy, and the Living Water is free for the asking, "Let anyone who is thirsty come. Let anyone who desires drink freely from the water of life." (Revelation 22:17)

"I am the Alpha and the Omega—the Beginning and the End. To all who are thirsty I will give freely from the springs of the water of life." (Revelation 21:6)

One of these days, each of us will leave this fallen world and head into eternity. For those who have accepted Jesus, the Living Water, it will be a joyful, glorious day! Our thirst will be satisfied!

Challenge: Take a few minutes to ask the Lord to fill you with Living Water. If you already know Him, ask for a replenishing. If you don't know Him, a simple, sincere prayer is all that is needed to acknowledge our sinfulness, confess Jesus as Lord and Savior, and commit our lives to Him. Those who do so are then given access to the Holy Spirit and the Living Water that fully satisfies!

Loving God, fill us with your Holy Spirit, the source of pure Living Water, and quench our spiritual thirst for all eternity.

The God of Small Things and Small Beginnings

"He rescues and saves his people; he performs miraculous signs and wonders in the heavens and on earth." (Daniel 6:27 NLT)

My granddaughter Kaitlyn was faced with a dilemma. She wanted to play basketball, a commitment she had made to her North Hills Christian School team, and she wanted to go with her youth group to a winter retreat at Winter Place in West Virginia. The problem: her ballgame was in southeast Charlotte at 4 p.m. on a Friday afternoon, and her youth group at Trading Ford Baptist Church would be leaving our church in Salisbury 62 miles away at 6 p.m. Since she had an obligation to her team, she very reluctantly decided to forego the trip.

Her parents and I, however, wanted to enable her to do both; but it was questionable how we could help her. The game which would begin at 4 would take at least an hour, and the drive from the gym—62 miles away--on a Friday afternoon in rush hour traffic would surely take more than an hour.

Praying for the Lord's direction and help, we headed to the ballgame. The NHCS team played well and won the game. It was 5:01 p.m. An alert on my phone came up: "Heavy traffic. One hour thirty-four minutes home."

Wow! It would be impossible! Our finite minds could not see a way. My daughter-in-law Kandee spoke up: "We're going to make it. Let's pray."

And the praying began! As we hit the beltway around Charlotte, traffic was backed up. We sought an alternative route on our GPS—there was none.

We crept along for a few minutes, and then as if the Lord were parting the Red Sea, there was an opening in the traffic. All the way from Providence Road in South Charlotte to Exit 81 in Salisbury—62 miles--the cars just seemed to move out of our way. We reached our destination in one hour—without speeding. It was a miracle!

As we pulled in to meet the church bus, everyone stood in amazement. Lisa, one of the youth leaders, exclaimed, "We are truly amazed! We stood in the parking lot at the church as a group and prayed. I told the kids to get specific in their prayers, and they did! The Lord answered!" Yes, he did.

Now in the scheme of world events, this was a tiny matter. Yet in the eyes of 31 youth and their leaders, it was a big deal. They got to see first-hand the power of God's people when they unite in prayer:

"Again, I say to you that if two of you agree on earth concerning anything that they ask, it will be done for them by My Father in heaven. For where two or three are gathered together in My name, I am there in the midst of them." (Matthew 18:19-21 NKJV)

I know without a doubt that the Lord is concerned about everything in our lives. The Scriptures tell us to "pray without ceasing." (1 Thessalonians 5:17 NKJV). If we follow this command, then we should talk to the Lord about everything from seemingly insignificant matters all the way to those that seem monumental.

After all, who are we to determine what is a small issue versus a big one? Only the King of the Universe can see what is taking place behind the scenes and determine the course of the future.

I recently led a Bible study on Henry Blackaby's book, *Experiencing God*. In the book, the author explains that there are seven realities that form the foundation for truly experiencing the Lord and his power:

1. God is always at work around you.
2. God pursues a continuing love relationship with you that is real and personal.
3. God invites you to become involved with Him in His work.
4. God speaks by the Holy Spirit through the Bible, prayer, circumstances, and the church to reveal Himself, His purpose, and His ways.
5. God's invitation for you to work with Him always leads you to a crisis of belief that requires faith and action.
6. You must make major adjustments in your life to join God in what He is doing.
7. You come to know God by experience as you obey Him, and He accomplishes his work through you.

Kaitlyn, her family, her friends, and her youth leaders experienced God first-hand that Friday afternoon. We all saw for ourselves the power of prayer, and we came to know Him in new ways as we experienced His mighty presence.

Who knows, though, what the Lord will do with that one small answered prayer that Friday afternoon as we rushed to catch a bus to a youth retreat?

For me I saw an immediate result the following Sunday as Pastor Mike Motley preached a message on the power of prayer. He spoke about Elijah and his dramatic encounter with evil King Ahab (1 Kings

18). Now, that was a prayer of great magnitude when Elijah called down fire from heaven to consume his sopping wet sacrifice and show to everyone who is the real Lord of the Universe. That prayer was one that changed the course of history.

Following his sermon, Pastor Mike extended an altar call and people made their way to pray. A young mother of four whom I know to have some big issues in her life knelt at the altar to pour out her heart. Then from the corner of my eye, I saw a slender young teen slip up beside her and kneel to pray with her. I was surprised—but delighted—to see that it was Kaitlyn. My heart overflowed as I saw her tender expression of compassion.

On our way home from church, I commended her for her sweet gesture. Her response spoke volumes, "I really wish you wouldn't say anything about that. When you feel a tug from the Lord, you just have to act."

Umm! Too bad we don't all respond to that little nudge from the Holy Spirit. The world would be transformed if we just obeyed those little prompts!

In that brief instant, I thought of Paul's words to Timothy, "Let no one despise your youth, but be an example to the believers in word, in conduct, in love, in spirit, in faith, in purity." (1 Timothy 4:12 NKJV)

The words of Zechariah also took on new meaning:

"Do not despise these small beginnings, for the Lord rejoices to see the work begin." (Zechariah 4:9-11)

Challenge: What about you? Seen any miraculous answers to prayer? Add a note of thanks to your

Gratitude Journal as you thank the Lord for the mini miracles we take for granted each day.

God of miracles, large and small, thank you for hearing and answering our prayers and giving us God moments when we grow in our knowledge of You and Your ways.

Dressed in the Best

"Clothe yourself with the presence of the Lord Jesus Christ. And don't let yourself think about ways to indulge your evil desires." (Romans 13:14 NLT)

I guess I show my age when I ask my granddaughters Lauren and Kaity why anyone would spend good money on clothes with holes in them. It makes no sense to me. Neither does it make sense why you would buy pants two sizes too big so they can hang down around your hips making it necessary to either hold on to them or jerk at them constantly to keep them from falling.

On reflection, though, I can remember a few unusual styles common in my day—penny loafers and white socks, beehive hairdos for women, duck-tail haircuts for men, and tacky leisure suits.

I can remember spending hours when I was a teen making the perfect red poodle skirt. It was soooo cute! And I wore several crinolines so that it would stand out and show off the design. (Very uncomfortable and impractical.)

I suppose each generation has its own distinctive ways of dress. We spend tons of money and countless hours of our time worrying about our clothes, hair, the latest styles, etc.

Do you ever wonder what would happen if we spent just as much time on our spiritual appearance—our minds and our souls—as we do on the physical aspects of life?

Our Pastor Mike Motley at Trading Ford Baptist Church once preached about "putting on" the mind of Christ and why it's a matter of life and death.

"Those who are dominated by the sinful nature think about sinful things, but those who are controlled by the Holy Spirit think about things that please the Spirit. So, letting your sinful nature control your mind leads to death. But letting the Spirit control your mind leads to life and peace." (Romans 8:5-6)

One reason that the world is not drawn to Christ is that we as Christians look and act just like the world. There is no distinction. And I'm not talking about physical clothing—although I think immodest dress does not reflect well on a Christian lifestyle. I am talking about matters of the Spirit.

You may remember that the fruit of the Spirit includes love, joy, peace, patience, kindness, goodness, gentleness, faithfulness, and self-control. (Galatians 5:22)

When we reflect rather hatred, worry, unrest, impatience, unkindness, evil, harshness, unfaithfulness, and lack of control, we do not reflect the mind of Christ.

The Bible tells us that the Lord is not interested in the latest fads—the coolest clothes—or the most flattering hairstyles. Rather, He wants us to develop inward beauty.

"Don't be concerned about the outward beauty of fancy hairstyles, expensive jewelry, or beautiful clothes. You should clothe yourselves instead with the beauty that comes from within, the unfading beauty of a gentle and quiet spirit, which is so precious to God." (1Peter 3:3-4)

Sadly, we as Christians do not always remember this truth: We have the mind of Christ within us. When decision times come, we are equipped to make sound decisions that reflect Christ, but we often make bad choices that dishonor Him. How could that be? We let our own flesh—or Satan—lead us astray.

Peter, who knew a great deal about making bad choices, advised us:

"Prepare your minds for action and exercise self-control. Put all your hope in the gracious salvation that will come to you when Jesus Christ is revealed to the world." (1 Peter 1:13)

Pastor Mike had these excellent suggestions for preparing our minds for right choices:

1. Remember that our minds are a battlefield and we need to bring them under the control of God.
2. The battle is ongoing and will continue as long as we live.
3. Satan, the father of lies, uses many tactics as he attempts to gain control of our minds. He tells us lies like: "God doesn't love you." "People don't like you." "Life has no meaning." "There is no hope."
4. We need to take steps to keep focused in the right direction:

- Think about what we are thinking about. Are our thoughts pleasing to God?
- Be wise enough to know that our thinking has great bearing on our choices. Choose to bring our thought life under God's control.
- Be sure of what we think about Jesus. Have we accepted Him or rejected Him? Have we wisely chosen life in Him or sadly chosen death in self and Satan?

Challenge: What about you? Are you "dressed" appropriately for living in the world today—not just physically—but mentally, emotionally, and spiritually? Are you enjoying your holy—not holey—wardrobe?

If not, may I suggest a new "Tailor?" One who has a Garment that will never wear out. Never get dirty or shrink. Never go out of style. "And all who have been united with Christ in baptism have put on Christ, like putting on new clothes." (Galatians 3:27 NLT)

When you choose HIM, you will never be or look or act the same: "They looked to Him and were radiant; their faces will never blush in shame *or* confusion." (Psalm 34:5 AMP)

Loving God, Designer of all that is beautiful, please clothe us in Your glorious wardrobe and may the world see YOU in every dimension of our lives.

Chapter Five

God Moments When He Calls Us to Service and Obedience

"Then I heard the Lord asking, 'Whom should I send as a messenger to this people? Who will go for us?' I said, "Here I am. Send me.'" (Isaiah 6:8)

And the Lord Spoke in Mysterious Ways

"Truly, O God of Israel, our Savior, you work in mysterious ways." (Isaiah 45:15)

It was one of the most surreal experiences I can ever remember having. I took my coffee, gathered my Bible, I-pad, journal, and devotional books, and sat down on my sun porch in my usual place to read and meditate. I thought to myself that it was a perfect morning—65 degrees outside, low humidity, birds singing—just gorgeous.

Out of nowhere, a ray of sun burst through the trees outside my window and bathed my face with light. The sounds of the breeze intensified, and the rustling through the trees was mesmerizing. I glanced up and saw my reflection in the glass door in front of me. My face was glowing! It was literally glowing! I felt like I was in the very presence of the Lord and had a new appreciation for how Moses must have felt when he saw the burning bush. It was mystifying–almost frightening!

My hands shot up in the air in an attitude of praise. The sun continued to bathe me in its incredible rays. Though the morning was chilly, and I had goose bumps on my arms, I felt warm through and through. The Holy Spirit seemed to envelop me and to call to remembrance:

"Now we see things imperfectly, like puzzling reflections in a mirror, but then we will see everything with perfect clarity. All that I know now is partial and incomplete, but then I will know everything completely, just as God now knows me completely. Three things will last forever—**faith, hope, and love**—and the greatest of these is **love**." (1 Corinthians 13:12-13)

An inaudible but clear voice spoke, "Write." And I responded, "Lord, but what? What do I write? I already write!"

The light gradually moved away, and I sat spellbound.

What had just happened? Had the Lord of the Universe told me in very clear terms to write? I had gotten similar messages before but not this directly. Was this real or my imagination? Yet even the title of my journal, on further inspection, seemed to reassure me it was real, "With God All Things Are Possible." (Matthew 19:26)

Again, I asked, "What do I write?"

My I-pad was beside me on the table, and I picked it up to find and read for myself 1 Cor. 13:12-13. I put it back down on the table and tried to see my reflection in the glass again, but it had disappeared. Then without warning, the I-pad beside me began speaking aloud. I jumped to see what was happening as the voice spoke loudly and clearly: "If I could speak all the languages of earth and of angels, but didn't love others, I would only be a noisy gong or a clanging cymbal." (1 Corinthians 13:1)

I did not understand how the I-pad began speaking, but I scrambled to see if I could turn it off. Perhaps I had brushed it somehow and turned on the audio. I still cannot comprehend how the machine spoke, but I knew what I was to write about: God's love and his expectation that we love others!

And so, I began to write what I seemed to hear Him saying:

"Love for others has all but disappeared in your culture which is bent on hatred and selfishness. You are a rude people, intent on having your own way with no regard for others. You need to love others—not hate them. I told you very clearly in my Word how you are to behave."

Instantly a passage of scripture came to mind:

"One day an expert in religious law stood up to test Jesus by asking him this question: 'Teacher, what should I do to inherit eternal life?'

Jesus replied, 'What does the law of Moses say? How do you read it?'

The man answered, 'You must love the Lord your God with all your heart, all your soul, all your strength, and all your mind. And love your neighbor as yourself.'

'Right' Jesus told him. 'Do this and you will live!'

The man wanted to justify his actions, so he asked Jesus, 'And who is my neighbor**?'**

Jesus replied with a story: 'A Jewish man was traveling from Jerusalem down to Jericho, and he was attacked by bandits. They stripped him of his clothes, beat him up, and left him half dead beside the road.

By chance a priest came along. But when he saw the man lying there, he crossed to the other side of the road and passed him by. A temple assistant walked over and looked at him lying there, but he also passed by on the other side.

Then a despised Samaritan came along, and when he saw the man, he felt compassion for him. Going over to him, the Samaritan soothed his wounds with olive oil and wine and bandaged them. Then he put the man on his own donkey and took him to an inn, where he took care of him. The next day he handed the innkeeper two silver coins, telling him, 'Take care of this man. If his bill runs higher than this, I'll pay you the next time I'm here.'

'Now which of these three would you say was a neighbor to the man who was attacked by bandits?' Jesus asked.

The man replied, 'The one who showed him mercy.'

Then Jesus said, 'Yes, now go and do the same.'" (Luke 10:25-37 NLT)

In a world increasingly filled with hatred, bigotry, and racism, the Word is clear. We need to love those who are unlovable, those who are different, those who persecute us, and those who even despise us. **LOVE**!

My mind drifted back to Seoul, Korea, 1968, the day I learned first-hand the evils of prejudice and racism. I was getting off a bus after work heading to the little room we rented in the home of a Korean family. My husband, Gerry, was serving in the military, and I was working on base as a secretary. Korea was still struggling to rise out of the rubble of the Korean War.

As I descended the stairs of the bus, I saw a Korean man who was standing on the sidewalk with his back to me. Just as I passed him, he whirled around and urinated on me. I was terrified! Several months pregnant, I ran for my life down the street crying out and weeping as he laughed hysterically behind me. It was the most terrifying, humiliating experience I had ever had.

It would be years before I could tell anyone about my experience. I felt violated, humiliated, shamed. The man did not know me, but he had, I believe, degraded me merely because I was a white woman.

Much prayer and reflection on that experience brought me to better understand the evils of racism. Now, I could choose to hate people of other races because of that tragic moment, but the Lord has told me repeatedly that I should see beyond that experience to what he wants me to do–**love—not hate**. He even explained in his Word what love looks like:

"Love is patient and kind. Love is not jealous or boastful or proud or rude. It does not demand its own way. It is not irritable, and it keeps no record of being wronged. It does not rejoice about injustice but rejoices whenever the truth wins out. Love never gives up, never loses faith, is always hopeful, and endures through every circumstance...Three things will last forever—faith, hope, and love—and the greatest of these is love." (1 Corinthians 4-7, 13)

The Scriptures warn us that the Lord knows even our evil thoughts and will deal with them, "But if we disobey God, as the people of Israel did, we will fall. For the word of God is alive and powerful. It is sharper than the sharpest two-edged sword, cutting between soul and spirit, between joint and marrow. It exposes our innermost thoughts and desires. Nothing in all creation is hidden from God. Everything is naked and exposed before his eyes, and he is the one to whom we are accountable." (Hebrews 4:11-13)

One of my husband's favorite verses that he often quoted to our children comes from this passage in Corinthians:

"When I was a child, I spoke and thought and reasoned as a child. But when I grew up, I put away childish things." (1 Corinthians 13:11)

Perhaps it's time for all of us to put away our old, mean, hateful ways of thinking and do as Jesus commanded: **"Love the Lord your God with all your heart, soul, and mind and your neighbor as yourself."** (Luke 10:27)

Challenge: What about you? Has the Lord ever spoken to you in some unusual, mysterious way that caused you to question your reality and wonder what was happening around you? Has He ever challenged you to speak out on an issue and even share personal details of your life when it was uncomfortable to do so? Has he ever given you a message in an inexplicable way that you felt He wanted you to share with others? Write about it in your journal and ask the Lord to help you share it with just the right people. Pray that He will use your testimony to encourage others.

Precious Savior, help us to pour out love first to YOU and then to others just as you poured out your very life for us.

Invest Your Life—Don't Just Spend It!

"Teach us to realize the brevity of life, so that we may grow in wisdom." (Psalm 90:12 NLT)

"Life is like a coin. You can spend it any way you wish, but you only spend it once." (Lillian Dickson, independent missionary, author, public speaker)

After I broke my neck in a car accident and was forced to slow down to a crawl during my recovery, I finally learned what it meant to "Be still and know that I am God." (Psalm 46:10)

Contrary to my preconceived ideas about being still, I found that I liked it; and I committed to continue my lengthy quiet times with the Lord when I recovered. After reading the quote above from Lillian Dickson, I really wrestled with the whole issue of investing my life rather than just spending it. I think a brush with death causes us to rethink our values and our lives.

With my decision to give up my workaholic ways and carve out more time to spend with the Lord, the reality of my lifestyle gradually hit home. I was not using my time wisely! My days were unfocused and fragmented. I spent too much time in needless activities. I wasted too many hours on television and the computer.

Another dilemma: For years I had felt called to write. How could I rearrange my time to carve our several hours a day to listen to God and to write what I believed to be His responses? For someone constantly on the go, this would not be easy.

As I wrestled with how to use my time more wisely, a tool developed by Stephen Covey, author of *Seven Habits of Highly Effective People*, came to mind. * Covey divided tasks into four categories based on importance and urgency. He challenged his readers to evaluate where they spent their time. (S. Covey)

URGENCY

IMPORTANCE	High	Low
High	**1** Urgent **and** important Do it now	**2** Important **not** urgent Decide when to do it
Low	**4** Urgent **not** important Delegate it	**3** **Not** important **not** urgent Dump it

I realized instantly that I spend an enormous amount of time in the bottom two quadrants, some time in the top left, and very little in the top right. My writing was a top priority—important but not urgent. I needed to carve out time to do it—and stick with my plan. I needed to dump time wasters, ask others for help with the urgent but not important, stop procrastinating, and decide when I would do the important but not urgent—my writing.

During my search for answers, I had what I believe was a "divine appointment." Rick Grubbs, a traveling evangelist and creator of Life Changing Seminars, came to our church and shared some ideas for time management. One question he suggested we ask ourselves stuck in my mind:

1. ***What does God want me to do right now?*** Who needs my ministry today—a call, a visit, a card, a prayer? What can I do to eliminate the unimportant and useless things in my life so that I can spend more time on the important? What can I do today to move my important projects like my writing along—to break down big, overwhelming tasks into small "bites" so that I can "eat the elephant one bite at a time?" I began to see that it is better to spend a few minutes each day on the important than wasting that time on the insignificant.

A second question emerged that I believe helps greatly in clarifying the important:

2. ***What would Jesus do?*** In the 90's, people sported bracelets and t-shirts asking this question. While

the trinkets are dated, the question is not. Jesus spent his time in Quadrant 2—important and not urgent. He never hurried. He spent time—lots of it—in prayer. He delegated the urgent but less important to his disciples while He concentrated his time on the lost and hurting.

Finally, I added a third question:

3. ***How can God be glorified in my current situation?*** What does he want me to do or say to point the world to HIM? What sacrifices do I need to make? Jesus was faithful even to death on the cross to bring glory to God. Perhaps some of our most difficult situations and decisions are just that: opportunities to bring glory to God. Whether it was Jesus on the cross, Daniel in the lion's den, Paul in prison, Esther in the king's harem, or Mary Magdalene at the foot of the cross or at the tomb, their focus was on bringing glory to God—not on their convenience or comfort. After much prayer and deliberation and asking myself these three questions, I decided on three simple—but big—changes in my day-to-day activities:

    1. Eliminate daytime television and cut back on evening watching dramatically.
    2. Go to bed an hour or two earlier so that I can get up earlier and spend more time in prayer, meditation, Bible reading, and

writing before meeting the other demands of my day.

3. Consider the first hours of the day as sacred time to be spent quietly with the Lord—no interruptions.

Has the plan worked perfectly? No. Am I doing better with my commitment? Yes. Am I concentrating on investing my life and not just spending it? Yes!

Challenge: How about you? Spending too much time on the unimportant? Re-evaluate your life and invest it—don't just spend it! Write about it in your journal and then obey the "Still Small Voice." The blessings are immense—and eternal!

"Lord, remind me how brief my time on earth will be. Remind me that my days are numbered— how fleeting my life is." (Psalm 39:4) May I use whatever time I have for your glory.

Just Get in the Boat!

"Trust in the Lord with all your heart; do not depend on your own understanding. Seek his will in all you do, and he will show you which path to take." (Proverbs 3:5-6)

A white-water rafting trip had sounded like great fun when we had planned our trip to Colorado months ahead. The day arrived for the adventure, however, and I was fearful. Three days before boarding the plane for my week's vacation with ten other family members, I had injured my lower back and was having difficulty simply walking. Was it wise to raft down the Arkansas River and risk getting thrown out of the boat and experiencing greater injury? It was probably not, but I really wanted to go!

As we approached the river, our guide gathered us together and explained what to do if we fell out of the boat. Stay close to the boat, swim, float, but don't try to stand up. You might get your foot caught under a rock. OOH!

We had already signed a waiver that we knew of the dangers of the sport, but the question still loomed: Should I get in the boat?

After the guide made sure we had our life jackets tight enough, and he had shown us how to paddle forward and backward, he directed us to get in the boat. His last words: Follow my instructions, work as a team, and we will be fine!

Before putting one foot in the boat, however, I explained my back situation to him. His response? No problem! Sit right in the middle of the boat just in front of him, hold on with both hands, let my family do the paddling and I wouldn't fall out!

Off we went! I had a marvelous time! My guide took good care of us. He gave great instructions, and the one time we got stuck, it was he who got out of the boat to push us off the rocks.

Such is our spiritual journey. Jesus often calls us to "get in the boat" or "get out of the boat" and do something we know full well we cannot do within ourselves; yet we learn if we obey Him, the Lord guides us and takes care of us.

Peter and the disciples learned this lesson frequently. In one of their first encounters with Jesus, they had fished all night and couldn't catch a thing. Jesus got in the boat with them and told them to push out and try again, and they caught so many their nets began to tear. (Luke 5:1-11)

On another occasion, they were out on the lake at night when a storm came up. They were terrified and began to call out to Jesus. When he awoke, he calmed the storm. His question to them, "Why are you afraid? Do you still have no faith?" (Mark 4:35-41)

On a third occasion, Peter saw Jesus walking on water toward their boat, and he asked Jesus if he could walk out to meet Him. Peter stepped out of the boat and walked! When his trust faltered, he began to sink. "Jesus immediately reached out and grabbed him. 'You have so little faith,' Jesus said. 'Why did you doubt me?'" (Matthew 14:31)

On all three occasions, Peter could not accomplish a task when he tried to do it under his own power. As long as he trusted Jesus, his Guide, he accomplished much—from fishing to surviving a storm to walking on water. As soon as he doubted, though, he began to falter and sink.

Such was my experience with Eric, my guide. I trusted him, got in the boat, and he took care of me.

Why is it that we have no trouble trusting other people whom we do not even know but we are afraid to trust and obey the King of the Universe?

When will we ever learn that it's not about us and our abilities but about Him? When will we truly embrace the

Word that assures us that, "I can do everything through Christ, who gives me strength." (Philippians 4:13)

We just need to get in—or out—of the boat as the Holy Spirit directs. Then we will be able to accomplish much in his name! Peter finally learned that lesson and became a mighty leader of the early Christian church!

My rafting trip was great fun thanks to my guide Eric and my dear family who paddled the boat. Such is my journey with the Lord. As long as I trust and obey, He guides me and protects me. The trip turned out to be much more than a great time on a family vacation. It served as a wonderful reminder that I just need to get in the boat!

Challenge: How about you? Are you afraid to "get in the boat" and obey the Holy Spirit's instructions? Pray about your situations and ask for His instructions. Then follow. Take a few moments to write about your insights in your journal. Add to your gratitude list.

Loving Lord, forgive us when we fail to trust you and are afraid. Give us the courage and the will to obey and follow your guidance.

Discerning and Obeying the Voice of God

"The Lord your God will delight in you if you obey his voice and keep the commands and decrees written in this Book of Instruction, and if you turn to the Lord your God with all your heart and soul." (Deuteronomy 30:10)

How do you learn to hear and obey the voice of God? That was the question being discussed as I sat at a conference at the Cove Conference Center, listening to the Blackabys—Henry, author of *Experiencing God*, his son Richard, and his grandson Mike. While I mulled over what the scriptures said on the subject, one verse about Jesus, the good shepherd, jumped out:

"He calls his own sheep by name and leads them out. After he has gathered his own flock, he walks ahead of them, and they follow him because **they know his voice**. They won't follow a stranger; they will run from him because they don't know his voice." (John 10:3-5)

"Follow Him (Jesus) because they know his voice." Hmmm.

"Do I faithfully listen and obey?" I questioned myself.

"Well," I thought, "if I'm truthful I'm too much like Moses. I hear the Voice, but I don't always want to obey. I sometimes question, procrastinate, argue, or just plain ignore rather than jump to it."

"Oh, to be more like Isaiah or Samuel or Mary who obeyed instantly," I muttered to myself.

When the conference session ended, I arose and headed to my room. As I started down the steps, though, I heard the Still Small Voice saying, "Go ask Henry Blackaby to pray with you."

"Do what?" I asked. "Am I hearing you correctly?" To be honest, my first inclination was to walk away and dismiss the Voice.

Halfway down the stairs, though, I told my companion that I would be on later and headed back to find Mr. Blackaby. I found him sitting by the fireplace chatting with another person. As I approached him, he smiled warmly. We exchanged greetings, and then I boldly asked him to pray with me. I explained my prayer concern, and he prayed.

When I walked away, my steps were lighter. I felt an immense peace—first about the answer to my prayer request but also about my obedience. Far too often, as I have already said, I am too inclined to dismiss the Lord's direction or postpone acting until later. This time, I had obeyed quickly. I knew I had done the right thing. A sense of joy bubbled up inside me.

The next morning, I walked into the dining room and filled my breakfast plate at the buffet. Several seats were available—one with a group of people I had met while at the retreat, and others at an empty table. Again, the Still Small Voice seemed to be directing me—this time to the empty table. My companion Kaye and I sat down. Before long, another woman asked if she could join us.

She introduced herself. (I'll just call her Patty.) We made small talk, and I learned she had traveled several hundred miles to the conference. Then unexpectedly she began to share her powerful testimony of becoming "Mommy" when she was not yet six years old. Her mother, an alcoholic, abandoned her and her two younger siblings. Though her father was still in the picture, he was negligent, and she soon became the mother figure in the home. Life was hard.

As an adult, Patty decided to look for her mother whom she hadn't seen in years. She finally found her—she was very ill. Through God's grace, Patty forgave her mother and shared the Gospel with her. Because of her witness, her Mom accepted Jesus as her Lord and Savior before she passed away.

As I sat listening, I heard the Still Small Voice prompting me to ask her if I could write her story. Immediately, as if I had slapped her, she burst into tears. I was surprised—even shocked—until she told me, "You are the answer to prayer. I have been wanting to write my story but never felt comfortable with the idea. I almost sat down at the other table but felt the Spirit prompting me to join you. I am amazed!"

We were both amazed! It seems we met by divine appointment. I still get goosebumps when I think about how the Lord brought us together—two women from different states—to meet in a distant city and share stories of the Lord's miracles. I was dumbfounded as I headed for home.

Again, I had promptly obeyed the Still Small Voice and so had Patty. Today you are reading but a snippet of her story. Perhaps in the future her story will be told in a book—all thanks to our listening and obeying.

It makes me a little sad to think of the many blessings I may have missed because I did not obey quickly but drug my feet. Jesus said, "But anyone who hears my teaching and doesn't obey it is foolish, like a person who builds a house on sand. When the rains and floods come and the winds beat against that house, it will collapse with a mighty crash." (Matthew 7:26-27)

I don't know about you, but I don't want to be a fool! He also said, "Those who accept my commandments and obey them are the ones who love me. And because they love me, my Father will love them. And I will love them and reveal myself to each of them." (John 14:21)

Challenge: What about you? Want to hear the voice of God? Read the Word. Listen for the Holy Spirit's still small voice. Obey immediately. For further reading on the topic, I highly recommend Henry and Richard Blackaby's book, "*Experiencing God: Knowing and Doing the Will of God.*" It's life transforming!

Good Shepherd, help us to hear your still small voice, listen without questioning, and obey immediately. May we indeed obey your word which tells us, "Serve only the Lord your God and fear him alone. Obey his commands, listen to his voice, and cling to him." (Deuteronomy 13:4)

*Henry T. Blackaby, Richard Blackaby, Claude King. *Experiencing God: Knowing and Doing the Will of God Revised*. (Nashville, TN: B&J Books, 2008.)

When the Doctor Was Wrong— Dead Wrong!

"You must not murder." (Exodus 20:13)

On January 23, 2019, while we were in Gatlinburg on a winter getaway, our family celebrated my granddaughter Lauren's 22nd birthday. We had a wonderful time eating seafood chowder, sushi and cupcakes, shopping for bargains at the Tanger outlet, and playing card games called Hand and Foot and Sequence.

Lauren is a special young woman. Bright and beautiful, she is, more importantly, a strong Christian who exhibits God's love and the fruit of His Spirit to those around her.

As I look at her smiling face and listen to her cheerful voice, I am horrified to think that before her birth her doctors suggested to my son Jeff and his wife Stephanie that they abort her.

For some still unknown reason, Stephanie's blood work came back showing problems with the fetus when she was five months pregnant. Her doctor's office called her at work one morning and wanted her to come in right away—it appeared there was something wrong with her baby.

Terrified, Stephanie rushed to the obstetrician's office where she met Jeff. The doctor then performed an ultra-sound and advised them that their daughter would likely be born with either downs syndrome or spina-bifida. He suggested scheduling an immediate abortion or, at the least, amniocentesis.

To their credit, my brave son and daughter-in-law said, "No, it does not matter. We do not believe in abortion. If the Lord gives us a handicapped child, we will love her anyway."

At a follow-up visit, a second ultra-sound was performed; and a different doctor unexpectedly announced that, in his opinion, the baby appeared to be fine. Needless to say, for the remaining weeks of her pregnancy, there was this continuing apprehension that Lauren would have special needs when she was born.

Praise God, when she arrived, she was perfect. Though initially she was a timid little thing and cried a lot for her mother, she grew into a vivacious, outgoing teen who excelled in music and drama. Elected president of the student body at East Gaston High School, she was anything but "handicapped."

Today she is a college student who is studying to be an Occupational Therapist. Her goal? To help children with special needs. For some reason only God knows, He has given her a special heart for children with disabilities.

As I listen to the horrific news that New York has now approved late-term abortion, I am angry. As a Christian, I find abortion abhorrent! To think that a mere doctor wanted to suck the life out of my beautiful granddaughter sickens me.

According to the Charlotte Lozier Institute, "abortions performed after 20 weeks gestation, when not done by induction of labor (which leads to fetal death due to prematurity), are most commonly performed by dilation and evacuation (D & E) procedures. These particularly gruesome surgical techniques involve crushing, dismemberment, and removal of a fetal body from a woman's uterus, mere weeks before, or even after, the fetus reaches a developmental age of potential viability outside the mother. In some cases, especially when the fetus is past the stage of viability, the abortion may involve administration of a lethal injection into the fetal heart *in utero* to ensure that the fetus is not pulled out alive or with the ability to survive."

The Scriptures are clear. We are all created in God's image:

"So God created human beings in his own image.
In the image of God he created them;
male and female he created them." Genesis 1:27

We are not just blobs of tissue. We are human beings from the time of our conception. God created us with tenderness and with a plan for our lives:

"You made all the delicate, inner parts of my body
and knit me together in my mother's womb.
Thank you for making me so wonderfully complex!
Your workmanship is marvelous—how well I know it.
You watched me as I was being formed in utter seclusion,
as I was woven together in the dark of the womb.
You saw me before I was born.
Every day of my life was recorded in your book.
Every moment was laid out
before a single day had passed." (Psalm 139:13-16)

He created each of us for a specific purpose, just as He created the prophet Jeremiah:

"I knew you before I formed you in your mother's womb.
Before you were born, I set you apart

and appointed you as my prophet to the nations."
(Jeremiah 1:5)

The 10 commandments are also clear:

"You shall not murder." (Exodus 20:13 NKJV)

As far as I am concerned, any doctor who would suck a baby from its mother's womb before it is full term or pump poison into its heart to destroy it is a murderer!

While I never considered myself a political activist, I have come to believe that the failure of Christians to take a stand for what is clearly contrary to the Bible's teachings is one reason our country is in such a state of moral rot and decay. Unlike the loud liberal protesters, we have remained quiet, and our children and grandchildren are suffering the consequences. It is time that we speak out for the rights of the unborn. Our Savior called us to take a stand:

"Then Jesus said to his disciples, 'If any of you wants to be my follower, you must give up your own way, take up your cross, and follow me.'" (Matthew 16:24)

Challenge: What about you? Where do you stand on the issue of abortion? What is the Lord encouraging you to do about it? Spend some time in prayer and allow His Spirit to speak to you. Then follow His direction.

Wonderful Creator, give us the courage to stand up for what You say is right in a country where "right has become wrong and wrong has become right."

Plowing with Jesus

"In that day, the Lord will end the bondage of his people. He will break the yoke of slavery and lift it from their shoulders." (Isaiah 10:27)

Every spring, gardeners pull out their tractors and tillers and prepare to plant their flowers, fruits, and vegetables.

In thinking about gardening, I am reminded of my mother who loved to plant a huge garden. She enjoyed being outside, plowing, hoeing, and gathering her crops. Me? I hated it! I learned early to cook, clean, wash clothes and dishes, and hang clothes on the line—anything to avoid the garden!

I can remember one time when she wanted my brother Ron and me to help her pull her little tiller. The plow was not designed to be pulled by children, but she apparently decided she could turn us into little mules. Well, that lasted about an hour! Neither of us was cooperative in the least and she gave up on the idea.

Shortly after that fiasco, my Dad bought her a gas-powered Merry Tiller. That thing was a beast! To my mind, there was nothing "merry" about it! Mother was a small woman, and I can still see her manhandling that tiller out through her garden! It was all she could do to keep it going in a straight line!

The entire idea of plowing was not something I cared to do! Perhaps that's why the passage from Matthew 11:28-30 has always been something of a paradox to me. "Then Jesus said, 'Come to me, all of you who are weary and carry heavy burdens, and I will give you rest. Take my yoke upon you. Let me teach you, because I am humble and gentle at heart, and you will find rest for your souls. For my yoke is easy to bear, and the burden I give you is light.'"

I liked the first part about rest, and doing anything with Jesus was always appealing; but in some ways I did not understand the imagery. How could plowing be easy?

The real picture became much clearer, however, when I accompanied five young residents of Capstone Recovery Center and their executive director, Miriam Ramirez, to Hickory Church of the Nazarene to celebrate Capstone Day. The young ladies were to share their testimonies. Before they began, however, Pastor Kyle DeLong preached a powerful mini-sermon on Matthew 11:28-30.

A yoke, Pastor Kyle explained, is a piece of equipment used to harness oxen, horses, or other animals so that they can effectively pull a wagon or a plow.

When training an ox or a mule, the farmer will often pair the inexperienced animal with a more experienced one so that the more experienced will teach the younger how to plow. The more experienced also carries the load as the younger walks along beside him.

My mind wandered to the powerful image of being rescued from sin and the legalism of Jesus' day and then being teamed with Jesus. Good news! He carries the load. He listens to Father God who is directing the team in the right direction. There is, indeed, rest for one's soul!

A horrific image also came to mind as I thought of being yoked to one of Satan's minions as he pulls one deeper and deeper into sin. Driving that team would be Satan himself. Sadly, this is the plight of lost people throughout the world.

As I looked around the sanctuary that Sunday morning and saw the beautiful, joyful faces of five young women who had been rescued by Jesus, I was teary. What a glorious picture of God's grace! The Lord rescued them and is now carrying their loads!

As a volunteer and board chair at Capstone, I find Psalm 126 very meaningful:

"When the Lord brought back his exiles to Jerusalem,
it was like a dream!
We were filled with laughter,
and we sang for joy...
Yes, the Lord has done amazing things for us!
What joy!...
Those who plant in tears
will harvest with shouts of joy.
They weep as they go to plant their seed,
but they sing as they return with the harvest."

When we founded Capstone Recovery Center several years ago, the Lord led us to plow in fields filled with addiction and hopelessness—not with wooden plows but with the Word of God. Even yoked to Jesus, the work has sometimes been hard. There has been weeping at times. But oh, the joy that comes with the harvest! Tears may fall, but at harvest time they are tears of joy! To see the faces of these beautiful young women—their new lives ahead of them—filled with fresh opportunities—is a glorious experience!

And now, as I sit here writing, another image from the farm comes to mind. We need more workers. My pastor at Trading Ford Baptist Church, Mike Motley, preached on this passage last Sunday. Jesus said, "The harvest is great, but the workers are few." (Mathew 9:37)

*Dwight Pentecost explains it this way:

"To take Christ's yoke means to submit oneself to the authority of Christ. It means to put ourselves under his rule, to join together with Him. He is inviting people to put their shoulders into a new yoke, one in which he is the yoke mate. And he promises that, as they submit to his authority and are yoked with him, they will find rest for their souls.

The yoke to which Christ invited people, when borne as a co-laborer with Jesus Christ, is no burden at all. It is a source of rest, satisfaction, enjoyment, and contentment. Christ is our life and he is our strength. When one is yoked to Jesus Christ, that which is performed is the joy of the true disciple...

Many of us have no right to call ourselves disciples. When we've heard Christ's words, 'Come to me, all you who are weary and burdened, and I will give you rest,' we have responded and have come to him. But when he prepares to slip a yoke around our necks to join us to himself, we resist, we fight, we back off. We refuse to be brought under bondage to anyone, not even to Jesus Christ. But until we become yoked to him in the sweetest bondage that heaven or earth knows, we cannot be disciples. 'Take my yoke upon you' means learn of me, submit to my Word, acknowledge the authority of my person. When we do that, and only when we do that, will we 'find rest' for our souls."*

Challenge: What about you? Have you found rest through being yoked to Jesus? Have you found the joy of "plowing" with Him and seeing the harvest He produces? There is nothing sweeter! If you are walking with Jesus as your yokemate, take time to thank Him and write about your experiences in your journal. If you have not yet submitted to Jesus, yield to Him and ask Him to walk with you throughout this life and into eternity.

Gentle Jesus, thank you for allowing me to walk with you as your yokemate. Help me to grow stronger and stronger in my faith as I learn from YOU.

**Dr. J. Dwight Pentecost was distinguished professor emeritus of Bible Exposition and adjunct professor in Bible Exposition at Dallas Theological Seminary before his death.*

Plugging in to the Power Source

"Jesus stood and shouted to the crowds, 'Anyone who is thirsty may come to me! Anyone who believes in me may come and drink! For the Scriptures declare, Rivers of living water will flow from his heart.' (When he said "living water," he was speaking of the Spirit, who would be given to everyone believing in him.)'"
(John 7:38-39)

For my birthday, my granddaughter Kaity gave me a little fountain. She was very excited as she pulled it out of the box and assembled it—a small tray for water, the fountain itself sitting on the tray, a power cord to plug it into the wall.

As I peered at it, I could not help but notice that it was plain and gray—nothing exceptional about it. But then she plugged it in, and the water began to flow. In addition, a light came on from deep within it.

Suddenly, it was beautiful! The bubbling water was so soothing that I placed it on my sun porch where I could turn it on and listen to it during my early morning Bible reading and meditation.

A few days later, I opened *Jesus Always*, a favorite devotional book. One passage was from John 4:13-14, an account of a conversation Jesus had with the Samaritan woman at the well:

"Jesus replied, 'Anyone who drinks this water will soon become thirsty again. But those who drink the water I give will never be thirsty again. It becomes a fresh, bubbling spring within them, giving them eternal life.'" (John 4:13-14)

My thoughts went back to my bubbling fountain. Without being plugged in to the power source, it was bland and colorless. Plugged in to the electric current, it came alive with moving water and bright light.

John 8:12 tells us, "Jesus spoke to the people once more and said, 'I am the light of the world. If you follow me, you won't have to walk in darkness, because you will have the light that leads to life.'" (John 8:12)

Wow! Living water that permanently quenches spiritual thirst flows from Him. Light that dispels the darkness of a sinful world emanates from Him. What beautiful imagery of what happens to us as Christians. When we choose Jesus, we plug in to His power. He fills us with "living water" that pours forth to those around us. He also fills us with "light" that banishes the surrounding darkness.

That's just what Jesus does for us when we accept Him and plug in to Him as our power source. We are transformed from bland to beautiful! We become a source of light and living water to those around us. The world is pointed to Jesus as we live and work and go about our daily business.

"With joy you will drink deeply from the fountain of salvation!" (Isaiah 12:3)

The goal of the Christian life is to point others to Jesus. What better way than to lead them to the real Power Source, the real Living Water, the real Light of the World! The "Light" prophesied in Isaiah that became a reality in Jesus Christ?

Isaiah prophesied: "The people who walk in darkness
will see a great light.
For those who live in a land of deep darkness,
a light will shine." (Isaiah 9:2)

I saw a great movie that dramatically portrayed the need for Christians to stay plugged in to the Power Source in order to live abundant lives.

In the movie *Grace Unplugged*, the lead character who was a gifted Christian musician, walked away from her Christian roots for the world of fame and fortune. Though she soon became successful in the world's eyes, she was miserable. It was only when she returned to the Lord and got plugged in again to His Power that she found true joy and happiness.

Challenge: Are you "plugged in" to Jesus? Have you chosen Him as your Power Source? Are you living the abundant life He wants for you? Or have you chosen to "unplug"? If you have never accepted Jesus or you have disconnected from Him, I beg you to reconsider. Choose the Source of Living Water! Choose the Light! You won't be sorry!

"We now have this light shining in our hearts, but we ourselves are like fragile clay jars containing this great

treasure. This makes it clear that our great power is from God, not from ourselves." (2 Corinthians 4:7)

Gentle Jesus, draw us close to you, our source of Light and Living Water, and use us to draw others to you so that they, too, can be "plugged in" to the Source of eternal life.

Can You Hear the Heavens Singing?

"I am leaving you with a gift—peace of mind and heart. And the peace I give is a gift the world cannot give. So don't be troubled or afraid." (John 14:27)

It was almost summer. Time to open the swimming pool. As we pulled off the old cover—worn and beginning to tear in places—I was shocked. The water was brown! An awful shade of brown. What had happened over the winter to cause this mess???

A quick check of the Internet revealed the problem. "The brown staining in your pool is probably caused by oxidized iron, which is getting in your pool from the well." Made sense. I'd been having problems in the house with dingy water. Guess all that water we put in the pool from the well last summer oxidized over the winter.

Notes to self: Big expense to fix. Another headache. What to do.

The next morning, I sat down in a fretful mood. It was shortly after dawn, and as I opened my Bible and devotional books, I was whiny. The sight of the brown pool below my window was disgusting. The problem was bigger than 30,000 gallons of brown water in what looked like a cesspool. I needed either an expensive water treatment system or a new well. Neither alternative was attractive.

I began to pray, "Lord, I'm in a bit of a mess here. What should I do?"

When I opened my journal, He gave me his answer. The scripture at the top of the page jumped off the page at me:

"For the Lord your God is living among you. He is a mighty Savior. He will take delight in you with gladness. With his love, He will calm all your fears. He will rejoice over you with joyful songs." (Zephaniah 3:17)

"Oh, Father. I need You to calm my fears. I do."

As His very presence began to quiet my soul, I began to ponder the last part of the verse and asked myself a question: Just how does he rejoice over us with joyful songs? Is that real or just spiritual?

Then I heard it! The birds and the crickets and the ducks on the lake were waking up. They were warming up their beautiful voices. It was like a heavenly choir.

As the sky turned pink and orange and yellow, the curtain rose on a new day—just like it has for thousands of years. The heavenly choir—the Lord's angelic voices broke the dawn. It sounded like a symphony. For over an hour I heard them, and then they quieted as if the Conductor had lowered the baton. The last few voices faded. The concerto was over until tomorrow.

Oh, the calm I felt! Yes, the Lord does "rejoice over you with joyful songs." He does calm our fears. The problem is we don't pause long enough to see, hear, or listen to what is going on around us. We are too consumed with the problems—big and small—in our lives.

A familiar passage came to mind:

"That is why I tell you not to worry about everyday life—whether you have enough food and drink, or enough clothes to wear. Isn't life more than food, and your body more than clothing? Look at the birds. They don't plant or harvest or store food in barns, for your heavenly Father feeds them. And aren't you far more valuable to him than they are? Can all your worries add a single moment to your life?...So don't worry about tomorrow, for tomorrow will bring its own worries. Today's trouble is enough for today." (Matthew 6:25-26, 34)

An overwhelming sense of calm filled my spirit. The Lord was looking after those birds, and they were singing their hearts out, seemingly in praise to Him. They weren't worried about tomorrow—and I shouldn't be, either.

What's 30,000 gallons of brown water? The Lord who made the water can surely make it clear!

Challenge: How about you? Have you heard the heavens singing lately? Has the Lord comforted you in your distress and troubles with music from His creation? If so, write about it in your journal and add it to your gratitude list. If not, pray and ask the Holy Spirit to make Himself known to you in His mysterious ways.

Holy Comforter, thank you for loving us and caring for us. Forgive us when we take you for granted. Help us to see, feel, and hear your mighty presence drawing us to your Peace.

Chapter Six

God Moments During Special Occasions and Holidays

"And people should eat and drink and enjoy the fruits of their labor, for these are gifts from God." (Ecclesiastes 3:13)

Searching for "God Moments" at Kure Beach

"Let all the earth be silent before him." (Hab. 2:20)
"Be still and know that I am God." (Psalm 46:10)

An early riser, I crept around in the Kure Beach condo where we were vacationing, trying to keep from awakening my sleeping family. With Bible, devotional books, and coffee in hand, I sat down at the kitchen table and began my morning quiet time with God.

I silently prayed, "Lord, what would you have me share with your children during our family devotions this morning?"

My first thoughts came from Joni Eareckson Tada's book, *Pearl of Great Price*. "Find time today to get outside, even if you have to wrap up warmly...Take in the beauty around you...Be still before God in wordless worship." (Psalm 46:10)

The meditation from Sarah Young's *Jesus Calling* next caught my attention. "Try to view each day as an adventure, carefully planned out by your Guide...A life lived close to Me will never be dull or predictable. Expect each day to contain surprises."

Ooh! What about a Scavenger Hunt—a search for "God moments" and miracles in unusual places or situations!

When I shared the two meditations at breakfast, I couldn't tell if my audience was listening, but I challenged them anyway to be alert to unusual ways they saw God at work during the day and report back any special "God moments" the following morning.

Bundled up in heavy coats and gloves, we spent the morning learning the history of Fort Fisher and observing a Civil War reenactment. During the afternoon, we walked on the beach, played shuffleboard, and warmed up in the hot tub. During the evening, we cooked seafood and played games at my grandson Luke's and his wife Hayley's apartment. It was a very pleasant day for a winter beach trip.

Exhausted, I headed to bed early—something I later regretted.

Sunday morning quiet time arrived. *Jesus Always* led me to Psalm 139, a favorite psalm that emphasizes the omniscience, omnipresence, and omnipotence of God and his unending love for us—his creation.

Um! A light bulb moment! Asking my family to look for "God moments" had been very shortsighted. Since God is omnipresent, there is no place where he cannot be found! Miracles abound all around us if we just open our senses!

When we reassembled for breakfast and family devotions, I was eager to hear their reports of special encounters with God, but I was also eager to tell them of my new insights.

One by one they shared their "God moments"—walking by the ocean and observing afresh the many colors of blue in the water and the sky, watching the glorious sunset off Fort Fisher, walking barefoot in cold, wet, sand while experiencing God's "grounding," listening anew to the power of the crashing waves, staring in amazement at the trees that have grown at a near 45-degree angle because of the wind.

All agreed, however, that the most unusual "moment" had occurred about midnight—after I had gone to bed—when Lauren, my granddaughter, and her boyfriend, Nick, heard a noise below our deck. On inspection, they discovered three deer searching for food—an unusual spectacle indeed in a resort area right on the beach. Jeff, my son who is well acquainted with deer, commented that it was the largest doe he had ever seen. The others agreed.

Deer sightings, I might add, are special in our family. On more than one occasion they have showed up in unusual places and under unusual circumstances—almost as if God sends them to us as a reminder that he gives power to the weak and is our source of strength in difficult times.

"The Sovereign Lord is my strength!
He makes me as surefooted as a deer,
able to tread upon the heights." (Hab. 3:19)

After each witness to the unusual deer sighting had commented on the experience, I asked them to listen as Lauren read Psalm 139 and reflect on their "assignment" once again.

"I can never escape from your Spirit!
I can never get away from your presence!
If I go up to heaven, you are there;
if I go down to the grave, you are there.
If I ride the wings of the morning,
if I dwell by the farthest oceans,
even there your hand will guide me,
and your strength will support me." (Psalm 139:7-10)

"If God is everywhere, why are we often so unaware of Him and His activities?" I asked. "Why do we notice only the unusual or spectacular? Why don't we recognize His presence in things we see every day?"

Their responses mirrored my own thoughts: We are too self-absorbed to see Him and His works. His miracles are all around us, but we take them for granted. We just don't pay attention.

The conversation finally turned to our previous day's visit to Fort Fisher—the site of the last major naval battle of the Civil War. Two more sobering questions arose. First, "What 'God moments' did the soldiers experience as they fought and tried to kill each other?" Second, "What was God doing and thinking when the peace and tranquility of this beautiful place was interrupted by cannons and gunfire?"

We discussed the fact that approximately 500 men were killed, wounded, or maimed in the battle. Many on both sides of the conflict were no doubt Christians who thought they were doing what was right. How did they see, hear, and experience God's presence in those wretched hours?

Our conclusion: God was there in January 1865 just as He is every day. He was probably doing what only God can do—binding up the broken-hearted, welcoming sons into heaven, and grieving over the pain, struggles, and sins of His children. The men engaged in the battle probably experienced Him just as we do today—Comforter, Savior, Divine Physician, Lord.

Our challenge today: To become more aware of His presence in the routine, every day events as well as in the spectacular by allowing Him to burst into our reality and reveal Himself to us—to open our eyes, ears, and hearts to Him in the many ways He speaks to us.

In the meantime, I can't help but hum the old hymn "Open My Eyes that I May See" written in 1895 by Clara Scott. Perhaps it would be a wonderful prayer for all of us:

"Open my eyes, that I may see
Glimpses of truth Thou hast for me;
Place in my hands the wonderful key
That shall unclasp and set me free.
Silently now I wait for Thee,
Ready my God, thy will to see,
Open my eyes, illumine me,
Spirit divine!" (Public Domain)

Challenge: What about you? What "God moments" and new insights have you experienced? Why not write about them in your journal and share them with someone who needs encouragement? If you have not experienced His presence, ask Him for a new revelation. He has promised to answer: "Keep on asking, and you will receive what you ask for. Keep on seeking, and you will find. Keep on knocking, and the door will be opened to you." (Matthew 7:7)

Abba Father, open our eyes to the wondrous world you have provided and the many ways you seek to communicate with us through special "God moments." May our souls thrill at your presence!

The Unwanted Mother's Day Gift

"Stay alert! Watch out for your great enemy, the devil. He prowls around like a roaring lion, looking for someone to devour." (1 Peter 5:8)

As I walked into my kitchen in search of my first cup of coffee, I knew something unpleasant was up! My cat, Puddy Tat, an 18- pound Maine Coon with a history of hunting and bringing unwanted critters into my house, was hunkered down and staring at something on the floor in front of him. Immediately, I feared the worst—he had somehow brought me a Mother's Day present that I would not want. Despite trying to keep a vigilant eye on him as he comes and goes outside, I sometimes fail, and he slips things past me or hides them on the porch when I'm not looking.

I was not prepared, though, for this "gift"—an 18-inch copperhead snake that lay at the edge of my counter coiled up and ready to strike my annoying cat!

Jumping back, I headed to the basement for a shovel. On my way, I awoke Jeff, my sleeping son who was visiting with me for Mother's Day, yelling for him to come quickly as I ran past his room. "There's a snake in the kitchen!" I yelled as I hurried down the stairs.

I grabbed the shovel and headed back up to the war zone, arriving before my sleepy son could make it up the steps.

I never thought I had it in me, but I slammed that snake, spraying blood across my freshly mopped floor while thinking to myself, "You won't be getting between me and my coffee again!"

A temporary moment of fear turned into laughter as I earned a new nickname—Shirley the Slammer. Both Jeff and I were amazed that I could kill anything—but I did.

On a serious note, though, that snake reminds me of how easily the first known serpent—Satan—weaseled his way into Eve's life. He was in her way then, too, as she headed for breakfast. Too bad she didn't slam him—instead of stopping to chat. The Scriptures tell us to "flee evil." We'd all be much better off if she'd just run as fast as she could!

Too bad we today don't recognize evil creeping into our lives. We have no problem identifying a real snake coiled up about to strike us—but we can't recognize the Serpent in our path when he comes calling, offering us some "forbidden fruit" or wanting to move in with us! Sadly, though, that "visit" can turn into an eternity in hell with other "snakes" just like him!

The Scriptures really don't tell us to slam him. Rather, they tell us to use our one defensive weapon—the one Jesus used when tempted in the wilderness—the Word of God. (Matthew 4:1-11) (Ephesians 6:11-17)

I pray I have the wisdom the next time I'm approached by the Evil One to slam him with the Scriptures rather than stop and chat like Mother Eve. Following the example of our Savior when he was tempted, it is better to hit him where it hurts:

"Then saith Jesus unto him, 'Get thee hence, Satan: for it is written, Thou shalt worship the Lord thy God, and him only shalt thou serve.'" (Matthew 4:10 KJV)

Or, if you like a modern translation:

"Get out of here, Satan," Jesus told him. "For the Scriptures say, 'You must worship the Lord your God and serve only him.'" (Matthew 4:10 NLT)

Challenge: What about you? Have you had a visit from the Serpent—Satan—recently? Do you know what to do if he visits? Do a word search on www.biblegateway.com and check out what the Scriptures tell us about encounters with Satan, the Devil, the Evil One. Spend some time praying for divine intervention when you encounter him again.

"Our Father in heaven,
May your name be kept holy.
May your Kingdom come soon.
May your will be done on earth,
as it is in heaven.
Give us today the food we need,
and forgive us our sins,
as we have forgiven those who sin against us.
And don't let us yield to temptation,
but rescue us from the evil one." (Matthew 6:9-13)

'Twas the Night Before Jesus Came

***"And she brought forth her firstborn Son, and wrapped Him in swaddling clothes, and laid Him in a manger, because there was no room for them in the inn."* (Luke 2:7 NKJV)**

It was time to close our weekly Celebrate Recovery meeting when she walked down the aisle and asked if she could share something. Not knowing what she might have in mind, I reluctantly agreed, praying it was appropriate.

Slowly she pulled a folded sheet of paper from her back pocket and began reading. As she continued, I was stunned. My thoughts were scattered. "How sobering!" I thought. "What do I do now with this parody of an old family favorite?" After all, I read the original poem to my children and grandchildren. They loved it.

For days, my mind returned to the poem and its implications. It jolted me to my core. I pray you will read it and share it with those you love.

'Twas the Night Before Jesus Came

'Twas the night before Jesus came and all
through the house
Not a creature was praying, not one in the house.
Their Bibles were lain on the shelf without care
In hopes that Jesus would not come there.
The children were dressing to crawl into bed,
Not once ever kneeling or bowing a head.
And Mom in her rocker with baby on her lap
Was watching the Late Show while I took a nap.
When out of the East there arose such a clatter,
I sprang to my feet to see what was the matter.
Away to the window I flew like a flash
Tore open the shutters and threw up the sash!
When what to my wondering eyes should appear
But angels proclaiming that Jesus was here.
With a light like the sun sending forth a bright ray
I knew in a moment this must be The Day!
The light of His face made me cover my head
It was Jesus! Returning just like He had said.
And though I possessed worldly wisdom and wealth
I cried when I saw Him in spite of myself.
In the Book of Life which He held in His Hand
Was written the name of every saved man.
He spoke not a word as He searched for my name;
When He said, "It's not here," My head
hung in shame!
The people whose names had been written with love
He gathered to take to His Father above.
With those who were ready He rose without a sound
While all the rest were left standing around

I fell to my knees, but it was too late;
I had waited too long, and this sealed my fate
I stood and I cried as they rose out of sight;
Oh, if only I had been ready tonight.
In the words of this poem the meaning is clear;
The coming of Jesus is drawing near.
There's only one life and when comes the last call
We'll find that the Bible was true after ALL!
Source unknown

Last Christmas as all my family gathered for our annual celebration, I tearfully read them the poem. I also told them that I could think of nothing sadder than getting to heaven and finding that one of them was missing.

Challenge: What about you? Do you need to share the "reason for the season" with your loved ones? Perhaps you need to share your testimony. Or perhaps you need to accept Jesus as Lord and Savior before it's too late. He's waiting for you with the most precious gift you will ever receive!

Precious Savior, as we celebrate your birth, may we remember your death, burial, and resurrection. Thank you for coming to save us and offer us the gift of eternal life through simple faith in You! May we accept that gift with humility and gratitude.

Birthday Breakfast with the Trinity

"Behold, I stand at the door and knock. If anyone hears my voice and opens the door, I will come in to him and dine with him, and he with me." (Revelation 3:20 NKJV)

It was my birthday! As I sat down at the table on my sun porch where I spend my quiet time with the Lord each morning, I was joyful—almost giddy.

For the first time in several years, I felt great—no physical pain and no overwhelming sadness nor depression. "Thank you, Lord, that I can stand up and walk pain free and that I still have my mind most days." (The sound mind part might be debatable if you ask my family!)

"Thank you for carrying me through the dark days with the loss of Gerald (my husband), Garrett (my grandson), Ron (brother), and Gail (sister-in-law.) over the past three years. Thank you for your faithfulness during those difficult times."

The longer I sat there, the more aware I became that I was hungry. Then out of the blue, I wondered what it would be like to have a real physical breakfast with the Trinity. Would they appear at my table as three distinct beings—Father, Son, and Holy Spirit—or as one? What would I say—if I could say anything? What would we eat? Would we have fish like the morning Jesus ate by the campfire with his disciples?

It was a marvelous conversation as I "talked" with the Lord and imagined such a time of fellowship. My imagination went wild.

I first imagined one chair with Jesus sitting smiling at me. Then I imagined three chairs with God the Father at one end and Jesus on his right with the Holy Spirit at his left. I know the Holy Spirit is just that—Spirit—but in my vision, He had a chair.

I then imagined what I might say. Gratitude to each began pouring from my mouth. I babbled on like Peter on the Mount of Transfiguration when he wanted to set up three tents for Jesus, Elijah, and Moses (Matthew 17:1-11). I thought about jumping up and beginning to set things in motion like Martha when she was trying to prepare the perfect meal (Luke 10:38-42). I imagined myself just falling on my face in fear and awe like John on Patmos (Revelation 1:17) or Isaiah in the throne room (Isaiah 6:5).

My mind rushed back to a special dinner I attended several years ago. As we entered the darkened room, the place was filled with candles and beautiful decorations. Tables were covered with white tablecloths and angels. There was a separate small round table at the front of the room. It was beautifully set with an exquisite place setting like you might see for the bride and the groom at a wedding. There was a spotlight drawing attention to this place of honor. As we shared a time of prayer and thanksgiving, I kept glancing at the special chair at the head of the table, envisioning the physical presence of Jesus Himself.

Then truth jolted me back to reality as my cat jumped in my lap wanting a back rub. As we sat there in the morning's peace, I reflected on my imaginations and realized I do, indeed, have breakfast with the Lord every morning! No, I can't see Him, but He is there. He is the "Unseen Guest" at every table. He is there when I quiet myself and listen to His still small voice. He is there when I'm rushing through the meal hastening to get on to one more project or one more event. He is there!

He is there as one God but in three distinct roles.

1. He is there as God the Father–First Person of the Trinity. Designer of all that is—including you and me. Architect of the universe.
2. He is there as Jesus Christ—Second person of the Trinity, who carries out the plans of the Father. The One who created what God designed. The One who died on a cross to carry out God the Father's plans to save us. The One who defeated Satan and will judge the world at the final judgment.
3. He is there as the Holy Spirit—Third person of the Trinity—the Breath of Heaven, the Force we feel within us that woos, guides, directs, and encourages us as we live as His followers, foreigners in a fallen world.

Another thought darted across my mind. Created in His image, we, too, are multi-dimensional. We, too, fulfill many roles. As for me, I have simultaneously been a wife, mother, daughter, teacher, ministry leader, and student.

Like the Lord, we have been given the capacity to design, facilitate, direct, and encourage, depending on the surrounding circumstances.

With new revelation and new understanding, I looked to the end of the table and in my mind's eye saw one chair and one God. I poured out my thanks to Him for designing me (Psalm 139), for loving me enough to die on a cross to save me from my sins (John 3:16), and for living all around and within me to direct me each and every day (Proverbs 3:5-6).

What a wonderful breakfast! Though I ate no physical food, I was filled up spiritually and emotionally. I will never sit down to do my devotions and see things in the same light. My birthday breakfast was life changing!

As a birthday present, I decided to buy myself a little gift—a reminder of my birthday breakfast with the Lord. It now hangs appropriately above my table where I meet often with the Lord—Abba Father, Brother Jesus, and Breath of Heaven.

The poem by Ken Brown says:

Our Unseen Guest

Within this home each day and night, we host a Special Guest, whose presence in so many ways shows how we all are blessed.

Not one but every room is shared and also every meal. Our guest is part of every prayer of thanks or quiet appeal.

This humble home immersed in love will now and ever be a little bit of heaven above. Our Unseen Guest is God, you see.

One of my favorite verses in the Bible sums up the mystery of the trinity:

"For unto us a Child is born,
Unto us a Son is given;
And the government will be upon His shoulder.
And His name will be called
Wonderful, Counselor, Mighty God,
Everlasting Father, Prince of Peace." (Isaiah 9:6-7 NKJV)

Challenge: What about you? Ever thought of the Unseen Guest in your home? Ever had a meal with Him? Take time at your next meal to engage the Holy Spirit. Imagine His presence. Talk with Him as you would any guest. Write about it in your journal. Add a note of thanks to your Gratitude List.

Abba Father, Gentle Jesus, Breath of Heaven, thank You that though You are One, You are also triune, and we can experience YOU in many wonderful ways.

Triune God, we thank You that we can experience You in three dimensions—Father, Son, and Holy Spirit. Thank You for surrounding us with Your presence, even when we are unaware of You.

Words!

"And the Word became flesh and dwelt among us, and we beheld His glory, the glory as of the only begotten of the Father, full of grace and truth." John 1:14 (NKJV)

Words. My weekend was all about words!

It started off on Friday with ***Stix and Stones***, a thought-provoking Easter drama at Central Triad Church in Winston-Salem that was far more than the usual Easter drama. Challenging words.

On Saturday I attended Barbecue and Oldies at Trading Ford Baptist Church, a benefit for an upcoming Honduras Mission trip that featured Mike and the Mustangs singing songs from the 50's and 60's. Old words.

On Sunday I attended church and then joined a group of 14 women as we traveled to Greensboro for Chris Tomlin's Holy Roar concert. Lots of words.

It was that first event—***Stix and Stones***—that really got me thinking about the importance of words. We're all familiar with the childhood rhyme, "Sticks and stones may break my bones, but words can never hurt me."

Well, the theme of the play confronted me with the truth: Words can hurt. Words start riots. Words destroy relationships. Words start wars. Words get people killed.

Just ask Jesus, Paul, Peter, and countless people today who are facing execution for their words.

Ever thought about the fact that it was His words that got Jesus killed? Had He never preached or spoken out against the religious leaders or if He had recanted his claim to be the Messiah, He probably would not have been crucified.

Because of words, Jesus' followers suffered and died. James was beheaded, Peter was martyred (probably crucified upside down), Stephen was stoned, Paul was beheaded, John was, according tradition, boiled in oil and miraculously survived to write the Revelation—and on and on.

Through the centuries countless Christians have died because of words. John Hus was burned at the stake in 1415 for criticizing the doctrines of the Catholic Church. John Wycliffe was so hated for his criticism of the Catholic Church and for daring to translate the Bible into English that his body was exhumed after his death and burned.

William Tyndale died at the stake in 1536 because he translated the Bible into English so that people could read and understand the scriptures for themselves. Words!

Fast forward several centuries, and words became extremely important to the founding fathers of this country. Protection of the right to speak was so important that the first amendment to our constitution reads:

"Congress shall make no law respecting an establishment of religion or prohibiting the free exercise thereof; **or abridging the freedom of speech, or of the press**; or the right of the people peaceably to assemble, and to petition the Government for a redress of grievances."[1]

Sadly, I fear our right to freedom of speech is taken for granted along with our other rights which are covered under this amendment—freedom of religion and freedom to assemble. Though we may not like what people say, we should protect their right to say it.

To be complacent on this issue can be deadly as evidenced by the execution of Christians in other countries simply for sharing their faith or choosing Christianity over other religions.

As I reflect on everything I experienced in my three-day weekend, I am thankful for many things. I am thankful that I could freely exercise my faith. I am thankful that I could say what I wanted to say and assemble in churches and concert halls without fear of persecution.

I am thankful I can read my Bible in English for myself. I am thankful that bold priests, prophets, and apostles like John were willing to risk their lives to write WORDS!

If we are to remain free in every sense of the word, we MUST stand up and speak up for our rights. And we must elect people who will stand up for us! Our first amendment rights are much too precious to let slip through our fingers for lack of attention or laziness.

1 https://www.history.com/topics/united-states-constitution/freedom-of-speech

The Lord told Joshua three times as he commissioned him to lead the children of Israel to claim the promised land:

"Be strong and courageous! Do not be afraid or discouraged. For the Lord your God is with you wherever you go." (Joshua 1:9)

That's what we must do: Be strong and courageous as we stand up and work together to make sure our government or our institutions do not take away any of our rights that our forefathers fought and died for. Though far from perfect, we live in a marvelous land, and we need to protect and keep it.

Chris Tomlin's Holy Roar concert wrapped up my weekend. His music and his lyrics—his words—were powerful. We as Christians can be strong and courageous because we have the God of Angel Armies on our side!

Jesus' last command to us his disciples emphasizes words:

"Go therefore and make disciples of all the nations [help the people to learn of Me, believe in Me, and obey My words], baptizing them in the name of the Father and of the Son and of the Holy Spirit, teaching them to observe everything that I have commanded you; and lo, I am with you always [remaining with you perpetually—regardless of circumstance, and on every occasion], even to the end of the age." (Matthew 28:19-20 AMP)

Yes, words are essential to carrying out the commands of Jesus, the Word! Let's use ours for His glory and protect our right to speak them freely for future generations.

Challenge: What about you? Ever sat down and reflected on the power of words? Ever wondered why Jesus called himself the "Word?"

"In the beginning [before all time] was the Word (Christ), and the Word was with God, and the Word was God Himself." (John 1:1 AMP)

The WORD—Jesus himself. The Alpha and the Omega is THE WORD!

Why not spend some time in prayer thanking the Lord for his Word and asking for guidance on what you should do to defend our freedom of speech? Consider writing in your journal your insights on how you use your words to carry out the Great Commission. (Matthew 28:19-20)

Dear Jesus, help us stand up and defend our right to speak freely so that never again will Christians die as You did for speaking truth! Help us share the Gospel message with those around us who do not know You as Lord and Savior.

Two Earthquakes and Then Came Sunday!

"So when the centurion and those with him, who were guarding Jesus, saw the earthquake and the things that had happened, they feared greatly, saying, "Truly this was the Son of God.'" (Matthew 27:54)

"And behold, there was a great earthquake; for an angel of the Lord descended from heaven and came and rolled back the stone from the door and sat on it." (Matthew 28:2 NLT)

The rain was coming down in torrents! I'd never seen such heavy rain. We stopped twice because of near-zero visibility. Water stood on the highways, making it dangerous to drive. It was about three in the afternoon on Good Friday—about the time Jesus died hundreds of years ago.

"How appropriate," I thought, as I sat there in the horrific storm and reflected on the scene following Jesus' death. I could only imagine what the people experienced during the earthquake. I'm sure they were terrified, just as we were on the highway as lightning flashed across the sky. As the earth shook following Jesus' death, the Roman soldiers at the foot of the cross finally recognized the truth!

"Then Jesus shouted out again, and He released his spirit. At that moment the curtain in the sanctuary of the Temple was torn in two, from top to bottom. The earth shook, rocks split apart, and tombs opened. The bodies of many godly men and women who had died were raised from the dead. They left the cemetery after Jesus' resurrection, went into the holy city of Jerusalem, and appeared to many people. The Roman officer and the other soldiers at the crucifixion were terrified by the earthquake and all that had happened. They said, **'This man truly was the Son of God!'**" (Matthew 27:50-54)

Even though the rain was relentless, and the winds were fierce, we finally made it to Myrtle Beach and got settled in for the week. Then came Rotten Saturday, as my Mother used to call it. Cold and very windy, it was not a good day to be on the ocean. Two red flags on the beach warned us not to be near the water. We stayed inside—and waited.

And then finally came Sunday! A glorious morning, we stood on the beach and watched the sunrise, singing "Amazing Grace" and reading the Scriptures about the second earthquake in the resurrection story:

"Suddenly there was a great **earthquake**! For an angel of the Lord came down from heaven, rolled aside the stone, and sat on it." (Matthew 28:2)

This earthquake, unlike the first, was a time for celebration! Jesus Christ was alive! He had risen from the dead! Good news!

With great joy in our hearts, a sausage biscuit in one hand, and a cup of coffee in the other, we next jumped in the car and headed to Wilmington—over an hour's drive away—for a nine o'clock worship service with my grandson Luke and his wife Hayley. It was truly a glorious time of worship at Life Point Church.

The message? **Reclaimed!** And how it resonated! That's what we are! Reclaimed and re-purposed for God's glory.

"He died for everyone so that those who receive his new life will no longer live for themselves. Instead, they will live for Christ, who died and was raised for them...**This means that anyone who belongs to Christ has become a new person. The old life is gone; a new life has begun!**" (2 Cor. 5:15, 17)

After church, we spent a wonderful day of fellowship with my precious family and headed back to Myrtle Beach. As we stood watching the moon rise over the now-calm ocean, I felt what the apostles must have felt when they finally grasped the truth: He's alive! He is risen! We can rest in His peace.

Challenge: Has Jesus rolled the stone away for you? Have you accepted His gift of salvation? Have you been reclaimed and re-purposed? Have you found your purpose—to bring glory to HIM? If not, I pray you run to Him and accept His forgiveness. Let Him remake you into the person He wants you to be and then celebrate your new life!

Precious Savior, we thank you for your death on the cross to save us from our sins. May we live our lives with great joy as your new creations, showing the world your power to transform lives from death to abundant life!

On the Wings of the Morning

"The faithful love of the LORD never ends! His mercies never cease. Great is his faithfulness; his mercies begin afresh each morning." (Lamentations 3:22-23)

It was a glorious morning at Myrtle Beach as we drove a few miles up Kings Highway to Brookgreen Gardens. My son Jeff and his wife Stephanie were taking me there for a belated birthday present. The first time I went to Brookgreen was on my honeymoon. That was many moons ago—1961 to be exact—and I was certain it had changed. I was right.

The welcome statue was the same, but beyond the entrance, it was quite different. Everything was organized. Tour guides escorted guests through the grounds and explained the history of the gardens. A boat ride took us out to the former plantations and rice fields. Animals and birds were abundant as the grounds are now a wildlife preserve.

We even saw a fox squirrel—a creature I had never seen before! Strange looking little fellow! Larger than most squirrels, he had a black mask. Cute!

Next, we took a tour of the grounds. There were hundreds of stunning views and wonderful statues, many no doubt taking years to create in the hands of world-renowned sculptors.

Then I saw it—my very favorite of all the 2,000 pieces there! The Wings of the Morning! One of my favorite chapters in the Bible—my go-to chapter when I'm feeling insignificant or discouraged—is Psalm 139. Marshall M. Fredericks had captured verses 7-10 in bronze. Amazing!

"I can never escape from your Spirit!
I can never get away from your presence!
If I go up to heaven, you are there;
if I go down to the grave, you are there.
If I ride the wings of the morning,
if I dwell by the farthest oceans,
even there your hand will guide me,
and your strength will support me." **(**Psalm 139:7-10)

All week following our visit, my mind drifted back to the message captured so beautifully in the sculpture sitting atop a reflection pool—man held in God's palm as he and two swans fly into the morning! Magnificent! A bit of internet research revealed that the sculptor had chosen swans because they are the Nordic symbol of spirit and symbolize eternal life. How appropriate.

Later in the week, as if in some mysterious response to our Brookgreen experience, our family soared into the heavens, too, as we took our very first helicopter ride. It was exhilarating.

Though afraid of heights, I had no fear. In fact, I thought it amusing that my granddaughter Kaity's t-shirt said, "Don't panic!" And I didn't. I envisioned myself resting in the hand of God—just like the man flying on the Wings of the Morning.

As we looked out at the beautiful sights and the ocean below, I was enthralled—not afraid. Psalm 139 resonated once again in my mind, and I was reminded that "if I go up to heaven, He is there. If I dwell by the farthest oceans, even there Your hand will guide me, and Your strength will support me."

What an awesome God we serve! He cares for us wherever we go—land, sea, sky! His promises say it all:

"For I hold you by your right hand—I, the Lord your God. And I say to you, 'Don't be afraid. I am here to help you.'" (Isaiah 41:13)

"See, I have written your name on the palms of my hands." (Isaiah 49:16)

What encouraging promises!

Challenge: What about you? Ever experienced the thrill of riding "on the wings of the morning?" If so, write about your experiences in your journal. Add your precious memories to your gratitude list. Share your experience with someone who needs encouragement.

Creator God, Gentle Savior, Breathe of Heaven, thank you for the thrill of resting in You, for the grand adventures we enjoy in Your marvelous creation, and for Your precious hand holding us tightly lest we fall!

Change Your Perspective!

"Instead, let the Spirit renew your thoughts and attitudes." (Ephesians 4:23)

Christmas was approaching, and there were two songs that I did not want to hear—too painful—"I'll Be Home for Christmas" and "Christmas in Dixie."

Beginning in late November one of them played on the radio often—too much. "I'll Be Home for Christmas." Written in 1943 to honor soldiers who longed to be home for Christmas, the song reminded me of my own bittersweet Christmas experience.

In 1967 my husband Gerry and I were in Seoul, Korea, where he was stationed with the Army. Communication during that time was limited to snail mail—no e-mail, cell phones, just letters. We were both 23 years old, and we had never been away from our families at Christmas. Living in a small rented room with a Korean family in downtown Seoul, we had each other but little else. Packages came in the mail, we opened them, and then we celebrated Christ's birth very quietly far from "home."

We did, however, look forward to Christmas 1968. Gerry would be discharged in October, and we would go "home." We would celebrate not only a change in location but also a new baby, for we had just learned we were expecting our first child. "I'll Be Home for Christmas" was a song of promise because we looked forward to a new life in a new home with family and friends and a new family member.

In time, we did go "home." Our first dear son Jeff was born in August 1968. Two other precious sons—Jonathan and Joe—followed. Our lives were full. We were, we thought, "home."

And then the years passed—almost 50 of them—and Gerry went "home" to heaven on January 10, 2016. Christmas would never be the same. I was a widow with cherished memories. "I'll Be Home for Christmas" now made me sad—not glad.

Another secular Christmas song that I dreaded hearing was "Christmas in Dixie." When the song was first published in 1982, Gerry was traveling with his job and often went to Fort Payne, Alabama, home of the singing group Alabama who performed the song. We loved the song and the group and often danced together when it was playing. It was, in some ways, "our" Christmas song. The thoughts of it now made me sad.

Christmas season, 2017, began before Thanksgiving. My favorite radio station played beloved Christmas carols often and secular Christmas songs occasionally. To my dismay, "I'll Be Home for Christmas" seemed to play every time I turned on the radio. Interestingly, though, "Christmas in Dixie" never played while I was listening—and I was relieved.

Then Christmas Day arrived. Our family celebrated with a time of Bible reading, worship and even the Lord's supper—traditions we practice as we try to keep our focus on Jesus and not on the world's commercialized ideas for celebrating this holy day.

We then shared Christmas dinner and headed to the living room to open gifts. My son Joe reached for the radio and turned up the volume just as I was getting ready to settle into my easy chair. To my utter surprise and dismay, "Christmas in Dixie" rang through the air. Suddenly grief stricken, I blurted out, "Turn that off, please!" Startled, Joe complied, but it was obvious that he was puzzled. A music lover, he wants music playing all the time. I think he was disappointed that our sharing of gifts took place in silence, but he said nothing.

As the family began to clean up wrapping paper and empty boxes, I felt I owed Joe an explanation. I went to him and shared why the song bothered me. To my amazement, he looked at me and with a keen sense of discernment whispered, "Mom, do you think it could have been something else? Look at it from another perspective. Perhaps it was a Christmas present from above," as he pointed upward.

I was flabbergasted. Had I missed a message from God? Could it be possible I was misunderstanding the events around me and failing to hear from Him because of a troubled heart and mind? Had He sent me messages of comfort that I had failed to receive? Was He reassuring me that, in time, I would be "Home for Christmas?"

Then for the first time all year, I allowed the refrain from Christmas In Dixie to wash over me, **"God bless you**

all, we love you, Happy New Year, good night, Merry Christmas." What a wonderful Christmas blessing—both here on earth and in heaven! And I almost missed it!

The following morning as I relived Christmas night and read my devotional meditations for the new day, the "Still Small Voice" seemed to give me three thoughts:

- First, my dear husband, Gerry, was "home" for Christmas, and one day I'll be moving there, too. "For we know that when this earthly tent we live in is taken down (that is, when we die and leave this earthly body), we will have a house in heaven, an eternal body made for us by God himself and not by human hands." (2 Cor. 5:1)

In fact, Jesus promised us, "Let not your heart be troubled; you believe in God, believe also in Me. In My Father's house are many mansions; if *it were* not *so*, I would have told you. I go to prepare a place for you. And if I go and prepare a place for you, I will come again and receive you to Myself; that where I am, *there* you may be also." (John 14:1-3 NKJV)

- Second, whether we live in Jackson, Mississippi, Charlotte, Caroline, or Fort Payne, Alabama, this is not our permanent home! We have a better place waiting for us, and we will move there one day! We are, in fact, "foreigners and nomads here on earth—looking for a better place, a heavenly homeland." (Hebrews 11:13, 16)

- Third, we as Christians are on "assignment" here in this world—just as we were in Seoul, Korea, that Christmas long ago. Jesus commissioned us, "Therefore, go and make disciples of all the nations, baptizing them in the name of the Father and the Son and the Holy Spirit. Teach these new disciples to obey all the commands I have given you. And be sure of this: I am with you always, even to the end of the age." (Matthew 28:19-20)

We have work to do! We are to be Christ's ambassadors in a lost and weary land. "God is making His appeal through us. We speak for Christ when we plead, 'Come back to God!' For God made Christ, who never sinned, to be the offering for our sin, so that we could be made right with God through Christ." (2 Cor. 5:20-21)

If you think about it, ambassadors serve all over the world in places not called home. In time, though, they do go home—just like we will one day! What a joyful thought! Home—with Gerry, Garrett, Mom, Dad, Joyce, Boyd, Dean, Jason, Mama, Papa, Gail, Ron, and countless loved ones already there—HOME!

In the meantime, we may need to change our perspective on what's going on around us. We may indeed need to view our circumstances with a renewed mind and attitude. To my delight, I am now humming "I'll Be Home for Christmas" and "Christmas in Dixie." What once brought pain now brings joy—for I see things from a quite different viewpoint!

Challenge: What about you? Has the Lord ever revealed something to you, and you missed the message until someone helped you see the bigger picture?

Do memories that once brought pain now bring joy because the "Still Small Voice" has changed your way of looking at them? Are there painful memories that you may need to see from a different perspective? Write about them in your journal. Are there memories for which you are thankful? Add them to your Gratitude Journal. Thank the Lord—and thank the people in your life—who help you see life with the Lord's perspective and not your own limited one.

Savior of the World, Breath of Heaven, Prince of Peace, thank you for the gift of discernment and for dear ones who help us see the Truth that will indeed set us free!

Chapter Seven

God Moments in Daily Living

"Lead me by your truth and teach me, for you are the God who saves me. All day long I put my hope in you." (Psalm 25:5)

A Glorious Rainy-Day Surprise

"Let all that I am wait quietly before God, for my hope is in him." (Psalm 62:5)

The flapping of wings drew my attention away from my journal where I was beginning my morning devotions. To my utter amazement, a squadron of 25 or 30 pelicans accompanied by blue herons and geese landed on High Rock Lake just outside my window. I was excited beyond description as I grabbed my phone and began snapping pictures. Who would ever have thought I would see pelicans on our fresh-water lake 200 miles from the nearest ocean?

The Lord, it seemed, had sent me a surprise on a dreary, depressing, rainy March morning—and I was as excited as a child over a new pet at Christmas! My spirits soared as He lifted me out of my gloom.

The surprise turned an ordinary, routine, mundane day into a wonderland! For several minutes I enjoyed watching the graceful birds swim up and down our cove, diving occasionally for fresh fish for breakfast.

Then what sounded like a gunshot rang through the air from somewhere in the distance. Just as suddenly as they arrived, their wings exploded into action as they soared into the sky and headed out in search of a safer location.

On two other occasions that month, my morning devotions were magically interrupted with the sound of wings. First came the pelicans, then several days later a raft of hundreds of mallards and later still a siege of black ducks. Each time the birds barreled into our cove, ate their breakfast, and took off in formation as they rounded the curve out of our neighborhood toward their new destination. What a blessing!

Several months earlier, the Lord had prompted me to slow down and leave behind my workaholic lifestyle and my tendency to worry over this world's "stuff," and I had tried to follow through on that commitment. Even though I am an impatient creature and want everything yesterday, I realized that is not God's plan. In fact, a fruit of the Spirit He has been giving me little by little is patience, because He knows that within myself, I just don't have it! What a blessing!

"The Lord is good to those who depend on him,
to those who search for him.
So it is good to wait quietly
for salvation from the Lord." (Lam. 3:25-26)

No, it is not easy, but I can say with great assurance that I have been immeasurably blessed as I have spent increasing amounts of time quietly waiting at his feet. Sarah Young, author of *Jesus Calling*, recently caught my attention:

"*Be still in My Presence, even though countless tasks clamor for your attention. Nothing is as important as spending time with Me. While you wait in My Presence, I do My best work with you: transforming you by the renewing of your mind.*" (Romans 12:2)

King David got it right. He was a busy man—a man on the run, a warrior, a king—yet he seemed to spend much time alone with God, rejoicing in his company, delighting in his presence, writing down his thoughts and prayers. Psalm after psalm share wonderful insights he gained as he sat with the King of Kings.

"Wait patiently on the Lord. Be brave and courageous. Yes, wait patiently for the Lord." (Psalm 27:14)

"You are my strength; I wait for you to rescue me, for you, O God, are my fortress." (Psalm 59:9)

"I wait quietly before God, for my victory comes from him." (Psalm 62:1)

Then one of my favorites:

"Take delight in the Lord, and he will give you your heart's desires." (Psalm 37:4)

I sometimes muse, "What does it mean to 'delight in the Lord?'" Do I spend enough time delighting in Him, adoring Him, and thanking Him for his wondrous gifts, or do I spend too much time just asking for "stuff"?

Perhaps we all need to ask, "Am I missing wonderful blessings because I am too busy, too worried, or too preoccupied to see what the Lord is trying to show me? Am I allowing the worries and concerns of this world to rob me of pure delight in the amazing gifts God is providing?"

Jesus gave us a clue as to one thing we can do to "delight in the Lord" when he encouraged us not to waste time worrying and obsessing over worldly concerns:

"That is why I tell you not to worry about everyday life—whether you have enough food and drink, or enough clothes to wear. Isn't life more than food, and your body more than clothing? **Look at the birds.** They don't plant or harvest or store food in barns, for your heavenly Father feeds them. And aren't you far more valuable to him than they are? Can all your worries add a single moment to your life?" (Matt. 6:25-27)

Challenge: What about you? Are you taking time to sit with the Master and receive His blessings? Are you allowing Him to transform your heart and your mind little by little, so you want what He wants? Or are you missing out on the wondrous "delights" He has to offer? Look around you! Be blessed! There is a glorious world filled with His blessings all around us if we but notice. Take a few moments to pray and add to your Gratitude Journal.

Holy Spirit, Breath of Heaven, thank you for your gifts—love, joy, peace, patience, kindness, goodness, gentleness, faithfulness, self-control—because within us we do not have them.

The Reluctant Giver

"You must each decide in your heart how much to give. And don't give reluctantly or in response to pressure. For God loves a person who gives cheerfully." (2 Corinthians 9:7)

Do you ever search the Scriptures for biblical examples of people who seemed to encounter circumstances like your own? I do. I love to see how biblical characters handled the crises in their lives and how God intervened in their situations.

Thus, it wasn't long after a potentially fatal car wreck that I began to search the Bible for anyone who suffered a broken neck—more specifically, a hangman's fracture. To my dismay, the most glaring example of such a person was Judas Iscariot who hanged himself after betraying Jesus. Judas, you may recall, betrayed Jesus for 30 pieces of silver. Then after realizing his sin, he took his own life because of his guilt rather than repenting and turning back to God.

Unlike Judas, my injuries were not self-inflicted; yet I still pondered whether I had anything in common with this villain.

Judas' sins, you may recall, were twofold: First, he was a betrayer: he led the Pharisees to Jesus and identified him with a kiss (Matthew 26:47-49). Second, he was driven by greed—30 pieces of silver to be exact. Money was more important to him than faithfulness to the One he had served for three years (Luke 22:3-6).

Greed. Umm. Do I have this problem?

In the process of self-examination, my mind drifted back to early September 2017, when I went to the bank to close a small account left to me by my late husband Gerry. As I entered the bank, the "Still Small Voice" gently prodded me: "You don't really need this money. You will never miss it. You should give it to your church (Trading Ford Baptist) for their September building fund campaign."

For several days after closing the account, I carried that check around in my wallet questioning the Lord, "Did you really say I should give this to the church? Really? You know, Lord, I could use the money, too." Finally, as the last week in September arrived and the building fund campaign neared its end, I wrote the check for the amount I received from the closed account and sent it to the church. I was keenly aware that the Lord "loves a cheerful giver" and I was working hard on my attitude, but if I am brutally honest, I was a somewhat reluctant giver.

Three weeks passed. October 23 arrived: car wreck—hospitalization—car totaled— (it was almost paid for)—looking forward to no car payments, now had to replace it—woe is me!

October 26, three days later, I got a call from a representative of my auto insurance company. She wanted to discuss the insurance settlement on the car. In my mind, I had already calculated an amount of money that would be equivalent to the value of my new car in 2014 minus three years of depreciation and 52,000 miles of use.

To my utter surprise, though, the agent began talking in terms of "replacement costs" and the fact that I had great insurance coverage (unknown to me but thanks to my insurance agent) and that I would be getting a sum that was several thousand dollars more than I had estimated! I almost fainted as I pinched myself to see if I were dreaming! I was amazed and delighted! When I received the settlement check several days later, it was for more than I paid for the car—the overage almost exactly equivalent to the contribution I had made to the Building Fund!

As I came to realize what had happened, I was amazed at the overflow of blessings I was receiving—all very much undeserved and unexpected! Because of this unforeseen blessing, I could buy a much better car than the one I was driving before the accident.

When I stepped back and realized the magnitude of blessings that Jesus pours out on me every day—all undeserved—I, like Judas, was guilt ridden. With great humility, I confessed my sin to the Lord and begged his forgiveness for my stinginess. After all, Jesus gave his very life on a tree for me—freely, at great cost! I had given a pittance to His church—reluctantly, even stingily—but he blessed me immensely, bountifully, abundantly—materially but also spiritually.

In reflecting on the events, two scriptures came to mind:

"People who conceal their sins will not prosper, but if they confess and turn from them, they will receive mercy." (Proverbs 28:13)

Too bad Judas didn't heed this.

"A thief (Satan) has only one thing in mind—he wants to steal, slaughter, and destroy. But I have come to *give you everything in abundance, more than you expect*—life in its fullness until you overflow!" John 10:10 (TPT)

The thief—Satan—fills our minds with evil desires just as he did in the Garden of Eden when he tempted Adam and Eve and in the Garden of Gethsemane when Judas betrayed Jesus. He wants to destroy us!

Jesus, on the other hand, wants to give us the abundant life both now and in eternity.

It's all about choice!

1 John 1:9_tells us, "If we confess our sins to him, he is faithful and just to forgive us our sins and to cleanse us from all wickedness."

Praise the Lord, I asked for forgiveness—and He provided it. I am grateful to Jesus for loving and forgiving me despite my weak, sinful nature!

Challenge: What about you? Have you experienced unexpected and undeserved blessings from King Jesus? Want to brag on Him? How about writing about it in your journal, add to your Gratitude list, brag on Him to others, and share your blessings with those in need.

Father God, Giver of all that is, thank you for every blessing you have generously poured out on us, and forgive us our stinginess. Help us to give freely and cheerfully as you direct.

The Sky Is Falling

"This is the day the Lord has made. We will rejoice and be glad in it." Psalm 118:24

As I staggered into the kitchen for my first cup of coffee, still half asleep, I saw it. There was a huge stain on my dining room ceiling that was getting darker and darker, and the sheetrock was beginning to peel off! I had a leak—and it was a big one!

In my mind, catastrophe loomed! As Chicken Little said, "The sky is falling! The sky is falling!" only it was not the sky, it was the roof and the ceiling!

It was too early to call a roofer so with coffee in hand, I tried to settle down at the dining room table for my quiet time—right in sight of the damaged ceiling!

Picking up a copy of *Daily Bread*, I sent up a silent prayer, "Oh, Lord," I prayed. "Help me get focused. Get my mind off the ceiling and on You." And He did—just not the way I expected!

"With a tendency toward pessimism, I quickly jump to conclusions about how situations in my life will play out," wrote Kirsten Holmberg, author of the day's *Daily*

Bread meditation. "Defeat in one area unnecessarily affects my feelings in many!"

"Oh, that's me, Lord," I confessed as I snickered to myself, thanking Him for how often He answers me as we talk each morning.

Then I read on. "It's easy for me to imagine how the prophet Habakkuk might have reacted to what God showed him. He had great cause for despair after having seen the coming troubles for God's people," Kirsten wrote.

Sobered by her confession and insights, I read the related scripture:

"Even though the fig trees have no blossoms,
and there are no grapes on the vines;
even though the olive crop fails,
and the fields lie empty and barren;
even though the flocks die in the fields,
and the cattle barns are empty,
yet I will rejoice in the LORD!
I will be joyful in the God of my salvation!"
(Habakkuk 3:17-18)

"Oh. my goodness!" I thought. Habakkuk was staring at real disaster, and I am complaining about a damaged ceiling and a leaky roof—things that can be easily repaired. He was facing the destruction of his country and exile to a foreign land, yet he was rejoicing in the Sovereign Lord. "Shame on me!" I thought as conviction flooded my soul.

"Oh, Lord. Forgive me for complaining about little problems! You have blessed me abundantly! Thank you! Help me keep things in perspective. This earthly roof can be repaired, and the roof in my heavenly home will never have holes in it! Thank you!"

As I tried to exit my pity party, I remembered the words of Jesus,

"Then, turning to his disciples, Jesus said, 'That is why I tell you not to worry about everyday life—whether you have enough food to eat or enough clothes to wear. For life is more than food, and your body more than clothing...These things dominate the thoughts of unbelievers all over the world, but your Father already knows your needs. Seek the Kingdom of God above all else, and he will give you everything you need. So don't be afraid, little flock. For it gives your Father great happiness to give you the Kingdom.'" (Luke 12:22-32)

"Oh, Father. You have spoken loud and clear. Forgive me. I am a believer, but I'm not acting like it. Thank you for helping me focus on what's important."

Remembering that an attitude of gratitude can do wonders in moving us from self-pity to a place of peace and joy, I grabbed my Gratitude Journal. As I began writing, an old song by Johnson Oatman, Jr., came to mind and I began to sing:

"When upon life's billows you are tempest-tossed,
When you are discouraged, thinking all is lost,
Count your many blessings, name them one by one,
And it will surprise you what the Lord has done.

Refrain:
Count your blessings, name them one by one,
Count your blessings, see what God has done!

Count your blessings, name them one by one,
**Count your many blessings, see what God has done."*
(Public Domain)

Challenge: What about you? Are you a worrier? If so, I urge you to grab your Gratitude Journal and start writing. If you don't have one, today would be a good day to begin. An inexpensive spiral notebook will do. Take time to add to it frequently, especially when "the sky is falling." It will help keep things in perspective.

Dear Jesus, forgive us when we disobey You and begin fretting over the problems of life. Help us to keep things in perspective and remember your many, many blessings.

In Need of a Tune Up?

"For we are God's masterpiece. He has created us anew in Christ Jesus, so we can do the good things he planned for us long ago." (Ephesians 2:10)

There it sat. It was almost 50 years old, and it had never been tuned. It looked fine on the outside, but it sounded terrible when it was played! It was not living up to its full potential. Even my 12-year-old granddaughter Kaitlyn knew something was wrong. "This piano sounds terrible. It is off pitch!" she had complained.

The doorbell rang and in walked the older gentleman who would restore it to its intended purpose.

For over an hour, he struck the keys and tightened the strings. When asked how he did it, he said, "I can just hear it...I've had years of practice...Started in 1955."

Finally, he put away his tools and sat down on the bench. Music filled the room—beautiful, breathtaking. Overwhelmed, I sat down to listen to the "master." What a privilege! The old piano had never ever had such glorious sounds emanate from it. The swell of "We Shall Behold Him," and "Edelweiss" filled the entire house. Tears filled my eyes so glorious was the music.

I had seen firsthand how the "master" had taken an old piano that had never been played by anyone but novices and young children and released it to make the sounds its creator had intended.

As the serenade ended and he left, I could not help but think of how we, as Christians, need the Master's touch to help us become all we can be. We don't enjoy being "tuned." "Stretching our strings" is painful but necessary for us to live up to the purpose for which we were created. "Tuning" may involve trials, troubles, and temptations or it may involve a call to do what seems impossible; but it is through these times of "stretching" that Jesus can use us for His glory if we but let Him.

Sadly, fear and lack of trust may cause us to refuse the stretching of the Master as we hold on tight to our old ways and patterns of living. Sometimes we think it is easier to stay in the safe routines of life rather than yielding to the Master's touch and call.

One of my favorite stories in the scriptures is of Moses and his burning bush experience. God was getting ready to stretch Moses mightily, but Moses was afraid. He used excuse after excuse trying to avoid God's call.

"But Moses pleaded with the Lord, "O Lord, I'm not very good with words. I never have been, and I'm not now, even though you have spoken to me. I get tongue-tied, and my words get tangled." (Ex. 4:10)

"But Moses again pleaded, 'Lord, please! Send anyone else.'" (Ex. 4:13)

Afraid, intimidated, content where he was, Moses did not want to follow the Lord's call.

I think I like his story so much because I can identify. When I was a high school senior, I fled an English classroom in tears because my voice quivered as I tried to deliver a report aloud, but I've learned since then that God uses the weak. He has a wonderful sense of humor. He took a timid girl and gave her a career in education and ministry where she had to talk. Who would have imagined it!

To this day, I still have a bit of stage fright when I speak, yet I am reminded of what Paul said about the thorn in his side and I am encouraged:

"Three different times I begged the Lord to take it away. Each time he said, 'My grace is all you need. My power works best in weakness.' So now I am glad to boast about my weaknesses, so that the power of Christ can work through me. That's why I take pleasure in my weaknesses, and in the insults, hardships, persecutions, and troubles that I suffer for Christ. For when I am weak, then I am strong." (2 Cor. 12:8-10)

As I reflect on what the master tuner did for my old piano, I am reminded of a beautiful poem written in 1926 by Myra Brooks Welch:

The Touch of the Master's Hand

'Twas battered and scarred,
And the auctioneer thought it
hardly worth his while
To waste his time on the old violin,
but he held it up with a smile.
"What am I bid, good people," he cried,
"Who starts the bidding for me?"

"One dollar, one dollar, Do I hear two?"
"Two dollars, who makes it three?"
"Three dollars once, three dollars twice, going for three,"
But, No,
From the room far back a gray bearded man
Came forward and picked up the bow,
Then wiping the dust from the old violin
And tightening up the strings,
He played a melody, pure and sweet
As sweet as the angel sings.
The music ceased and the auctioneer
With a voice that was quiet and low,
Said "What now am I bid for this old violin?"
As he held it aloft with its bow.
"One thousand, one thousand, Do I hear two?"
"Two thousand, who makes it three?"
"Three thousand once, three thousand twice,
Going and gone," said he.
The audience cheered,
But some of them cried,
"We just don't understand."
"What changed its worth?"
Swift came the reply.
"The Touch of the Master's Hand."
"And many a man with life out of tune
All battered and bruised with hardship
Is auctioned cheap to a thoughtless crowd
Much like that old violin
A mess of pottage, a glass of wine,
A game and he travels on.
He is going once, he is going twice,

He is going and almost gone.
But the Master comes,
And the foolish crowd never can quite understand,
The worth of a soul and the change that is wrought
By the Touch of the Masters' Hand.

If God is calling you to a task, He will prepare you—stretch you—to complete the task.

Twice Jesus told his followers that "anything is possible" through Him.

First, in speaking with his disciples, "Jesus looked at them intently and said, "Humanly speaking, it is impossible. But not with God. Everything is possible with God." (Mark 10:27)

And then, in speaking with a man who had brought his troubled son to Jesus for healing:

"'The spirit often throws him into the fire or into water, trying to kill him. Have mercy on us and help us, if you can.'

'What do you mean, 'If I can'?" Jesus asked. 'Anything is possible if a person believes.'

The father instantly cried out, 'I do believe, but help me overcome my unbelief!'" (Mark 9:22-24)

When we are afraid and filled with doubt, perhaps we need to remember the plea of this father: "I do believe but help me overcome my unbelief."

May we be like Isaiah who ran toward—not away—from God's call:

"Then I (Isaiah) heard the Lord asking, 'Whom should I **send** as a messenger to this people? Who will go for us?' I said, 'Here I am. **Send** me.'" (Isaiah 6:8)

Challenge: What about you? What is the Lord calling you to do? Will you allow Him to "stretch" you and enable you to live up to your full potential? Whether you consider yourself a grand piano or a violin or a toy ukulele, rest assured that the Master can tune you to perfection and use you as a part of the most beautiful orchestra that has ever been assembled! Spend some time today praying about how the Lord may stretch you and then yield to his call.

Gentle Jesus, give me courage to follow You even when I am afraid.

Taxes!!

"Give to everyone what you owe them: Pay your taxes and government fees to those who collect them and give respect and honor to those who are in authority." (Romans 13:7)

It was almost April 15, 2017, and I had finally gotten around to doing my taxes—frightful experience! In 2016, I received a sizable refund. In 2017, when Turbo Tax and I finished the dreaded deed, I owed many, many dollars! How could this be?

After much examination, I determined that the reason for the difference was that since my husband Gerry passed away in 2016, I could no longer file married but had to file single. It just didn't seem fair!

On a lighter note, some of our worst times together as a couple were as we sat down to do our taxes! Only the more "mature" among us remember pre-computer days when you had to spend hours and hours filling out tax forms by hand and calculating everything with a calculator! I'm sure if Gerry could look down from heaven, he would have been saying, "Thank you, Lord, that I don't have to be involved with her again in that experience!"

Seriously, though, this was no laughing matter! How could I owe more in income tax now that I was a widow, and I had less income coming in? Puzzling!

To make matters worse, the Lord and I "discussed" this problem for days. I raved and ranted, and He gently referred me to his Word. Matthew, Mark, and Luke all report an incident where Jesus said, "Pay your taxes."

"Well, then," he (Jesus) said, "give to Caesar what belongs to Caesar, and give to God what belongs to God." (Matthew 22:18-21, Mark 12:13-17, Luke 20:20-26)

Like a petulant child, I wanted a reprieve, but it did not come! My only other options were illegal or immoral, and I didn't want to choose those paths. The Word is clear about lying or stealing!

To add insult to injury, I opened www.biblegateway.com on my last day to procrastinate, and the verse for the day hit me between the eyes:

"Pay your taxes, too, for these same reasons. For government workers need to be paid. They are serving God in what they do. Give to everyone what you owe them: Pay your taxes and government fees to those who collect them and give respect and honor to those who are in authority." (Romans 13:6-7)

Hmm! "Government workers" need to be paid. Give respect and honor to those in authority. Was the Lord speaking to me? What was He trying to say? In a matter of a few short minutes, He confronted my "stinking thinking" with seven reminders of why I should just stop procrastinating and pay up:

First, He seemed to say, you enjoy living in the United States of America—the greatest country on the face of the earth. While it is flawed, it is still a country where you are free—free to complain openly about your taxes! To protect that freedom, we need a strong military. Taxes pay their salaries.

Second, as a retired teacher, you **were** one of those "government workers" for 30 years. Your daughter-in-law is a teacher today. Your very livelihood was paid for through taxes!

Third, you are the product of a free public education. Though our education system is also imperfect, you are the person you are today thanks to an education your parents could not have afforded to pay for.

Fourth, your current income is partially paid for through our Social Security System. Though also unsound, it is the primary method of support for millions of seniors.

Fifth, you, along with all seniors, enjoy low-cost health care. Though faulty, it is still available. When you broke your neck and had to be hospitalized, your bills were low thanks to Medicare and a supplemental health care plan.

Sixth, your taxes help provide food for many people who live on very meager incomes or have no income at all. Your taxes put food on their tables and a roof over their heads. Even though the welfare system is abused, it is still a means of providing for the poor, and the scriptures tell us to take care of the needy.

Seventh, Jesus loved tax collectors—just like He loves you and me! Tax collectors were considered notorious sinners in Jesus' day. All children in Sunday School learn about Zacchaeus, the wee little tax collector who climbed a tree to see Jesus. After Jesus went home with him for supper, he was saved and gave up his sinful ways. The apostle Matthew was another tax collector Jesus saved and then used to write an account of his birth, death, and resurrection.

While the IRS is not popular today, it is our current method of funding our government. If we don't like it, we can vote for new leadership and pray they change the system.

The bottom line: The Lord seemed to be telling me to stop complaining and pay my taxes! And so, I did! I wrote out my check—still a little reluctantly—but with gratitude rather than whining about it.

My only wish as I signed it: that I could do as Jesus did and send one of my sons down to the lake behind my house and catch a special fish!

"On their arrival in Capernaum, the collectors of the Temple tax came to Peter and asked him, 'Doesn't your teacher pay the Temple tax?'

'Yes, he does,' Peter replied. Then he went into the house.

But before he had a chance to speak, Jesus asked him, 'What do you think, Peter? Do kings tax their own people or the people they have conquered?'

'They tax the people they have conquered,' Peter replied.

'Well, then,' Jesus said, 'the citizens are free! However, we don't want to offend them, **so go down to the lake and throw in a line. Open the mouth of the first fish you catch, and you will find a large silver coin. Take it and pay the tax for both of us.'" (Matt. 17:24-27)**

Now that's what I call a perfect solution to a tax problem!

Challenge: What about you? Ever resent having to pay taxes? If so, take out your gratitude list and start writing. I'm sure your blessings outweigh your taxes.

Giver of All Blessings, thank you we live in a free country where we have the privilege of living the "abundant life" through You. Help us never to take our many blessings for granted, even as we pay our taxes.

Decisions, Decisions: What to Do When You Can't Decide

"We can make our own plans, but the Lord gives the right answer." (Proverbs 16:1)

Do you ever have trouble making decisions? I do. I can spend hours agonizing over things that are inconsequential. Sometimes I am even paralyzed by indecision.

There are occasions, however, when a decision must be made immediately. For example, I was at a writer's conference, and the choice of workshops was overwhelming. Before I had left home, I had carefully reviewed the schedule and selected what I thought I would attend. Faced with the final decisions, though, I ended up in a totally different direction. It was as if the Lord said, "Go this way," and I very reluctantly followed his lead.

I felt very much like Paul must have felt—on a much smaller scale, of course—when he reached the border of Asia and was redirected to go to Macedonia (Acts 16:6). Or Philip who was ministering in Samaria when he was redirected—quite suddenly—to a desert road headed to Ethiopia (Acts 8:26). Redirects can be unsettling, even scary. Thoughts like "What if I choose the wrong direction, Lord? What if a make a mistake?" always rush through my mind.

Eva Marie Everson, one of the speakers at the conference, pointed out that there are people in the Bible who argued with the Lord, and the consequences were not pleasant! Take Jacob, for example. He wrestled with God and ended up walking with a limp. Or Jonah. He went the wrong way entirely, and he ended up in a cold, dark place for three days!

I do not want to end up with a limp, and I don't want to be coughed up out of the belly of a stinking fish. I want to hear and obey! Decisions—even little ones—are important!

The bottom line: What if I make a wrong choice? That thought really plagues me.

The real issue, I suppose, is a lack of trust. Paul trusted the Lord and followed his direction without arguing or questioning. He trusted his Divine GPS.

The Scriptures reassure us, I think, that we can relax. Take Proverbs 19:21, for example. "You can make many plans, but the Lord's purpose will prevail."

I've read that verse many times and always found it a bit discouraging. To me it seemed to say that no matter what I planned or chose to do, it really didn't matter. The Lord would always have His way.

Much more comforting is my latest interpretation: I can plan and do my best to listen and follow, but if I do make a mistake, the Lord will take care of it—His plans will ultimately prevail.

I often think of one of my mother-in-law's favorite scripture passages, Romans 8:26-28: "And the Holy Spirit helps us in our weakness. For example, we don't know what God wants us to pray for. But the Holy Spirit prays for us with groanings that cannot be expressed in words. And the Father who knows all hearts knows what the Spirit is saying, for the Spirit pleads for us believers in harmony with God's own will. **And we know that God causes everything to work together for the good of those who love God and are called according to his purpose for them.**"

Hallelujah! I can relax! I can listen to the Still Small Voice, try to follow, and trust Him with the outcome! What an amazing promise that He is with us, interceding for us, directing, and even correcting our paths. In the end, His purposes will prevail!

Like Paul, who loved the Lord above all else, we can end up in the right place doing the Lord's will, even if it's not where we initially thought we should go. Also, though our decisions may seem like little ones compared to Paul's, even those little decisions can have big consequences. The Lord is interested in the little things and the huge ones. If He knows how many hairs we have on our heads, He is certainly interested in what we are thinking and what we are doing and where we are planning to do it (Matthew 10:30)!

Faced with a decision—a big one or a little one—I have determined to follow a simple 7 step plan:

1. Love the Lord.
2. Examine my circumstances.
3. Pray.

4. Listen to the Still Small Voice.
5. Choose.
6. Trust.
7. Relax. Ultimately His purposes will prevail—and that is an incredibly good thing!

This poem by Janet Wallace sums it up quite well:

GOD'S GRACE ENABLES ME

I know it's the Spirit
Who's at work within me
'Cause I don't do these things by myself.
I have tried, and I've tried,
But it's always the same.
On my own everything is a mess.
I give praise to my Lord.
I give praise to my King.
I give glory and honor to God.
For it's him and not me,
This I clearly do see.
It's His grace that enables me.

Challenge: What about you? Do you have any important decisions looming? Try the seven-step plan and see where the Lord leads. Then write about it in your journal. You may be amazed at where he leads and the glorious adventures that lie ahead!

Holy Spirit, Breath of Heaven, may we seek to follow your lead in decision making and earnestly believe that your purposes will be fulfilled if we but trust and obey.

What's So Special About Sparrows?

"Even the sparrow finds a home, and the swallow builds her nest and raises her young at a place near your altar, O Lord of Heaven's Armies, my King and my God!" (Psalm 84:3)

It was a dreary, rainy morning. Though there was still snow on the ground, it was no longer beautiful and white. Rather, it was streaked with brown as it had been melting for several days.

I sat down on my sun porch with a cup of coffee preparing to do my daily Bible study and meditation. Recovering from a sinus infection, I was in a "blah" mood. A familiar clang roused me out of my stupor, and I turned toward my bird feeder, hoping to see a beautiful cardinal. Instead, a platoon of sparrows took turns diving in for breakfast.

"Well," I thought, "even the birds are drab and brown. Nothing particularly beautiful about them."

As I stood watching the sparrows, I noticed how delicate they were. I also remembered reading about them in the Bible. Jesus was sending his disciples out on their first missionary trip without Him. He no doubt knew they were anxious and worried, and He reassured them:

"And do not fear those who kill the body but cannot kill the soul. But rather fear Him who is able to destroy both soul and body in hell. Are not two sparrows sold for a copper coin? And not one of them falls to the ground apart from your Father's will. But the very hairs of your head are all numbered. Do not fear therefore; you are of more value than many sparrows." (Matthew 10:28-31 NKJ)

"Well," I thought, "I know little about sparrows. Since Jesus talked about them and He considered them valuable, what can I learn?"

A bit of Internet research told me that sparrows are some of the most familiar and most common birds in the world. The term "sparrow" covers a wide range of relatively small, mostly drab brown birds, which birders often call "LBJs" or "little brown jobs" because they are so difficult to identify. In fact, there are dozens of different sparrow species throughout the world—over 50 of which are found in North America. Sparrows can be found on every continent except Antarctica. Their brown color serves an important purpose as it makes excellent camouflage.

Most sparrow species are relatively small, with sizes ranging from 4-8 inches. Amazingly, they weigh only .85 to 1.4 ounces!

As I reflected again on the "fun facts" about "little browns," I looked at them with new admiration. They could even sing—something I was not particularly good at. They could fly—I certainly couldn't do that. They are very adaptable, and they aren't hard to please. (Sometimes I am.)

They can also be very neighborly. According to The Spruce https://www.thespruce.com/what-is-a-sparrow-387102, sparrows are solitary or found only in pairs or family groups during the spring and summer breeding season. In autumn and winter, however, they will form mixed flocks of different sparrow species, and may even be mixed with some other small birds such as wrens or chickadees. Surprisingly, they sometimes build their nests so that the walls touch a neighbor's.

On a more negative note, however, they can be extremely aggressive. They will drive away other species and take over a bird feeder. Since they are considered by many birders to be a pest, there are even articles on how to get rid of them!

In retrospect, their behavior reminds me a great deal of us humans—loud, bullying, and territorial on one hand but neighborly and gregarious on the other.

As I walked back on the porch, another tiny bird caught my attention. He was sitting in my crepe myrtle bush beside the sun porch **singing**! How wonderful!

I watched in amazement, remembering that this delicate creature weighing slightly more than an ounce, lives, breathes, eats, flies—and sings!

My mind drifted back to Jesus' statement. Not one of these tiny birds can fall to the ground without His knowing it. That tiny sparrow is precious to the Lord. He is part of His wonderful creation. Yet He loves us more! What a comforting thought!

In the future, instead of desiring only to see the bright and beautiful, I will pay special attention to the ordinary sparrow. After all, that's what I am! An ordinary person with no great beauty or exceptional talent—yet the Lord knows all about me and loves me, anyway! He even knows how many hairs are on my head!

A final thought flitted across my mind as I picked up my Our *Daily Bread* devotional book: "Would there be sparrows in heaven?" I mused. Then I read the title of the day's meditation: "Heaven's Love Song"–Revelation 5:1-13. As I read verse 13, the Lord gave me my answer!

"And then I heard **every creature in heaven and on earth and under the earth and in the sea. They sang:**

'Blessing and honor and glory and power
belong to the one sitting on the throne
and to the Lamb forever and ever.'" (Revelation 5:13)

How wonderful to get to heaven and hear sparrows sing along with the people of God! They'll no longer fear us. We'll all be part of the same choir! Won't that be spectacular! Every human and every creature singing to the glory of God! It gives me goosebumps just to imagine the magnificence of such a never-ending cantata!

Challenge: What about you? Over the next few days, spend some time quietly watching the sparrows and birds in your neighborhood. Read what the Word says about birds. Contemplate what it will be like to join a heavenly choir made up of all creation. Sing a song of praise to the One who made it all!

Oh, Great Creator, thank you for the wonders of creation and all the amazing birds and animals you

placed in the world for us to care for, learn from, and admire. May we take our jobs as caretakers of your world seriously.

Afterword

Credit Where Credit Is Due

Jesus looked at them intently and said, "Humanly speaking, it is impossible. But not with God. Everything is possible with God." (Mark 10:27)

I think God gave me sons—particularly Joe, my youngest—to keep me humble. When Joe was four years old, I came home from passing my final exams in my doctoral program at NC State University. It was a big day, and I was excited. My older sons, Jon and Jeff, had made posters and greeted me with obvious applause. Joe, on the other hand, didn't seem too impressed. As the older boys returned to their activities, I tried to answer his questions and explain that I was not a medical doctor—that my degree was in Adult and Community College Education.

A few days later, I overheard Joe talking with five-year-old Chip, a neighborhood friend. Chip whispered to Joe, "Is your mother really a doctor?" Quite nonchalantly, Joe responded, "Yeah, but she can't doctor nothing and she don't have no white coat."

Fast forward several years, and Joe, then seven or eight years old, accompanied me to work at Central Piedmont Community College. I had just been promoted to dean of the business department, and in that role, I spent much of my time in meetings with faculty, students, and fellow administrators. Joe played quietly in the corner of my office much of the day—something unusual for a highly active little boy. When we got home, my husband Gerry asked Joe, "Well, did Mommy work hard today?" Joe's response, "No, not really. All she did was sit around and talk to people."

Believe me. If I ever had any inclination toward pride in my accomplishments, Joe took care of it!

In fact, all these many years later, he and his brothers are still full of mischief and enjoy a good time, often at the expense of each other or their Mother.

Since I began writing, though, I have had quite a few people make kind, supportive comments about what I had written. While I am pleased and flattered by the encouragement, I am reminded with great humility that all the credit goes to the Lord—and not to Shirley.

Countless times through the years the Lord has enabled me to do things that I never thought possible. Writing is just one of them.

From childhood, I struggled with low self-esteem. As a teen, I always felt very inadequate. As a senior in high school, I fled my senior English class in tears because my voice quivered so badly when I was trying to give an oral report that I was mortified.

While I was a student at Gardner-Webb University, I put off public speaking, a required course, until my last semester. Every speech I made, I over prepared. I was terrified every time I stood to speak. There was no deodorant strong enough to deal with my fear.

As a business and economics major, I envisioned myself working behind the scenes somewhere as a secretary until I had children and stayed home to raise them. But the Lord had different plans. In fact, He has a real sense of humor!

At the prodding of my husband and my mother, I transferred to Furman University where I minored in business education. Even though one of my favorite games as a young child was playing "teacher" to my little brother and my younger cousins, I never imagined I could ever teach because of my stage fright. How could I ever become a teacher if I couldn't speak in public?

As a senior at Furman University, I was required to take part in student teaching. Again, standing before a group of students was terrifying—but I survived. I was beginning to see that with God's help, I could do what seemed impossible.

When offered a teaching position upon graduation, I reluctantly took it. My first year was tough, yet I made it through and even began to relax a bit by mid-year and enjoy it.

As I look back over my life, I am still amazed that the Lord sustained me through 30 years as a teacher and college administrator! He took a most unlikely candidate for such a career and transformed her, bolstered her, and encouraged her.

I am reminded of Moses and Gideon—both filled with terror at the prospect of carrying out the Lord's plans. I know how they felt. I can identify with their fear and apprehension.

As I neared the end of my career in education, the Lord led me to retire and attend seminary. He kept calling me to begin a support group ministry. While I was again a student at Gardner-Webb University, this time in graduate school, He also led me to pastor a small church in Spartanburg for two years—something that was beyond anything I ever expected to do.

Upon graduation from Gardner-Webb, we returned home to Salisbury. I sat down in my easy chair with my new M.Div. and told the Lord that I didn't know why He had sent me off to the seminary. I told Him I was too old to be much use in traditional ministry and that I needed Him to send someone to my door to tell me what to do.

I never really expected him to do such a thing; but a few days later, Mike Motley, my former pastor at Trading Ford Baptist Church, knocked on my door and asked my husband Gerry and me if we would come back to his church and begin a ministry called Celebrate Recovery. Even though we had never heard of the ministry, we agreed to listen.

My circuitous path now made sense. My call to support group ministries became a reality. With an incredible team of people who also heard God's call, we began Celebrate Recovery, a ministry to people struggling with hurts, habits, and hang-ups. Later He prompted us to help start a Celebrate Recovery prison ministry at the women's prison in Troy, North Carolina, and then to help found Capstone Recovery Center, a Christ-centered transition home for women struggling with substance abuse.

TFBC's Celebrate Recovery Ministry will soon celebrate its 15th anniversary! Who except the Lord would ever have imagined it!

Now, back to writing. As early as 2011 the Lord began prompting me to write a book. Obviously, I am very much behind in obeying His call.

Yet I also know that His timing is not my timing! He knows me to be a procrastinator. In fact, I spent much of the past three years housebound because of a car accident where I broke my neck and then again when I had lower back surgery six months later and most recently in recovery from breast cancer surgery and radiation. When we are slow to obey, He helps us to "Be still and know that I am God (Isaiah 46:10)." Though very much inconvenienced, I can look back and see how those months enabled me to write.

In fact, during that difficult time, I started a blog which has become the basis for this book, and I began thinking about writing a second book—a collection of testimonies of people in recovery. Now, you may wonder when it will be finished. To be honest, I have no idea because they are HIS words and not mine. I will record them as He gives them to me—and not before.

For I am not a writer, but a scribe. I have found that He can use me to write if I let Him fill me with words—His words and not mine.

I read a devotional thought recently in Our *Daily Bread* entitled "Giving Credit." The emphasis was on giving God credit: "Let the one who boasts boast in the Lord." (1 Corinthians 1:31)

Jeremiah, the weeping prophet, said it well,

"This is what the Lord says:
'Don't let the wise boast in their wisdom,
or the powerful boast in their power,
or the rich boast in their riches.
But those who wish to boast
should boast in this alone:
that they truly know me and understand that I am the Lord
who demonstrates unfailing love
and who brings justice and righteousness to the earth,
and that I delight in these things.(Jeremiah 9:23-24)

Moses, Gideon, Mary Magdalene, the demoniac out in the tombs—all knew that without the Lord, they were useless in His kingdom.

James knew it, too: "So don't be misled, my dear brothers and sisters. Whatever is good and perfect is a gift coming down to us from God our Father." (James 1:16-17)

Bottom line: Thanks for reading this my first book. If you enjoyed it, know that it is the Lord who deserves any applause and any glory. I am only a reporter, but what joy I feel as I reflect on all the wonderful opportunities He has provided through the years!

Be on the lookout for the second book that the Lord has inspired me to write. Who knows, it may be completed before the second coming—it's all in His time! In the meantime, check out my blog at www.shirley-luckadoo.com. Thanks for reading.

Challenge: What about you? Can you look back and see the hand of God on your life in ways you never expected? Have you seen Him enable you to do what you thought was impossible? Take time to give praise where praise is due—at the feet of the Master Potter!! Write in your journal. Add to your gratitude list and thank him for revealing YOUR God moments! Then share, share, share what He is doing in your life with others.

God of the impossible, thank you for using us as your ambassadors to a lost and dying world. May everything we do and say be pleasing to YOU!

CPSIA information can be obtained
at www.ICGtesting.com
Printed in the USA
LVHW011616180521
687787LV00002B/148